AMERICAN CIVIL WAR ARTILLERY 1861–1865

FIELD & HEAVY ARTILLERY

AMERICAN CIVIL WAR ARTILLERY 1861–1865

FIELD & HEAVY ARTILLERY

TEXT BY PHILIP KATCHER • ILLUSTRATED BY TONY BRYAN

First published in Great Britain in 2001 by Osprey Publishing, Elms Court, Chapel Way, Botley, Oxford OX2 9LP, United Kingdom.
Email: info@ospreypublishing.com

Previously published as New Vanguard 38: *American Civil War Artillery 1861–1865 (1) Field Artillery* and New Vanguard 40: *American Civil War Artillery 1861–1865 (2) Heavy Artillery*

ISBN 1 84176 451 5

Editor: Simone Drinkwater

Printed in China through World Print Ltd.

01 02 03 04 05   10 9 8 7 6 5 4 3 2 1

FOR A CATALOG OF ALL BOOKS PUBLISHED BY OSPREY MILITARY AND AVIATION PLEASE CONTACT:

The Marketing Manager, Osprey Direct USA, c/o Motorbooks International, PO Box 1, Osceola, WI 54020-0001, USA. Email: info@ospreydirectusa.com

The Marketing Manager, Osprey Direct UK, PO Box 140, Wellingborough, Northants, NN8 4ZA, United Kingdom. Email: info@ospreydirect.co.uk

www.ospreypublishing.com

ARTIST'S NOTE

Readers may care to note that the original paintings from which the color plates in this book were prepared are available for private sale. All reproduction copyright whatsoever is retained by the Publishers. All enquiries should be addressed to:

Tony Bryan, 4a Forest View Drive, Wimbourne, Dorset BH21 7NZ, UK

The Publishers regret that they can enter into no correspondence upon this matter.

EDITOR'S NOTE

The images of woodcuts reproduced in this book are all part of the author's collection.

FRONT COVER: Pontoons were vital to the operations of both sides in the Civil War, for the first task of a retreating army was to destroy all bridges that could be used by the pursuing enemy. These Federal Troops are practicing a river crossing with artillery in a makeshift boat made of pontoons lashed together and covered with a log deck.

CONTENTS

INTRODUCTION

I n the 1860s, at the start of the American Civil War, American artillery experts were in the midst of a major change of direction. In the early years of the 19th century, American artillery had an overwhelmingly English influence, which stemmed from the War of Independence nearly a century earlier. At that time, the British army used 3-, 6-, 12-, and 24-pdr. light brass guns, carried on wooden carriages with split trails. During the War of Independence, the Continental Army received some French-made field artillery, 4-, 8-, and 12-pdrs. mounted on carriages that were very similar to those of the British. They also used Swedish-made 4-pdrs. that were utilized by the French Army as regimental close support weapons.

Although these weapons used brass tubes, the copper needed for manufacturing brass was scarce in America, while iron was plentiful throughout the country. Cannon foundries were located in both the north and south of the country before the Civil War, and after 1800 the American army almost exclusively adopted iron for making gun barrels. The exception was the American-designed "King Howitzer," which used a short brass tube with a 2 3/4-in. bore designed to shoot a grenade a short distance, a typical use for a howitzer. It was ideal for fighting Indians in the densely wooded northeast, but was of little use against organized forces using their own artillery.

After the adoption of iron, American-made artillery used the British caliber system of 6-, 12-, 18-, and 24-pdrs. instead of the French system. On the other hand, French carriage design was chosen over the British style. A series of M1818 "walking stick" cannon burst during tests in 1827, however, and a number of artillerymen began to lose trust in iron. The known brittle qualities of the metal, coupled with its weight, made it unsuitable for cannon tubes, they felt. In 1836, therefore, the Ordnance Board, after testing iron and bronze as barrel metals, decided that America's field pieces

Many batteries at the war's outset were armed with obsolete 6-pdr. cannon with iron tubes, such as this M1831 example. (Ft. McHenry National Park)

should thereafter employ bronze barrels. This ruling did not settle the question immediately, and both metals were used until a commission of ordnance officers toured European foundries, arsenals, and armories in 1840. On their return to the U.S. they reported, and the Ordnance Board confirmed, that bronze was the superior metal and would thereafter be the sole field artillery barrel metal.

In 1840 the U.S. Army adopted a French carriage, copied from a British design, that used a single rather than a split trail. The most common was the 6-pdr. gun carriage, used to mount the standard 6-pdr. iron gun and the 12-pdr. bronze howitzer. Eventually, this would become the standard carriage of the American Civil War for all field artillery (carriages for Napoleons had slightly separated cheeks to accommodate the greater tube diameter). At the same time a new limber and ammunition chest was adopted, the latter with iron handles so that cannoneers could ride on it while it was being transported. The limber was also used to pull newly adopted battery wagons and traveling forges.

The principle gun immediately before the Civil War was the 6-pounder which had been used to great effect during the Mexican-American War (1846-48) by mounted batteries in particular. Mexican artillery, which ranged from 4- to 16-pdrs. with mostly 8-pdrs. in the field, was not as mobile and therefore offered little in the way of effective counter battery fire against highly mobile 6-pdr. batteries. Moreover, Mexican artillery was poorly coordinated and fired mostly solid copper shot that was so slow in flight that the Americans were able to duck easily.

The war reinforced American belief in mobile field artillery, which meant at that point the 6-pounder. But the 6-pdr. had some real problems. The longest range at 5 degrees was 1,523 yards with solid shot, and 1,200 yards with spherical case. Artillerymen wanted a gun that fired heavier shot a greater distance. The 12-pdr. howitzer had the projectile weight, but not the range, since it was basically designed for close-quarter fighting. Moreover, it was relatively heavy, as it was not

The muzzle of a Napoleon made by the Columbus, Georgia, Arsenal bearing, clockwise from left, the inspector's initials, "C.S ARSENAL COLUMBUS GEO. 1864," and the weight of the tube. (Gettysburg National Battlefield Park)

intended to be a mobile piece but to be used in and around fortifications.

Much the same debate had been going on in France, resulting in a field artillery piece firing a 12 lb. shot, but with a bronze tube weighing only 1,200 pounds. A shorter weapon than the M1841 American model, it was an excellent field piece. The Ordnance Board quickly adopted a copy of this weapon, the Model 1857, as its standard weapon. It was officially known as the "Gun-Howitzer," the "Light 12-pounder," and the "12-pdr. Gun, Model 1857," but it was most commonly called the "Napoleon." Like a howitzer, it was able to fire shells or canister, although technically it was not a true howitzer because it was could also fire shot like a gun.

The Napoleon was adopted in 1857 but few were in use in the south before war shut down the borders. The Confederate arsenals and the local forts they captured were stocked mainly with 6-pdrs., and these made up their main field artillery power at first. The handful of guns available from the pre war military forces, (both the regular U.S. Army and some artillery militia groups) was so small that both sides would have to depend on their industries to supply the large volunteer armies needed to fight this war.

Moreover, the southern foundries had been making 6-pdrs. before the war and had the technology and expertise to continue, which was vital in getting a force armed quickly. With the expense of acquiring artillery overseas and the uncertainty of acquiring extra cannon on the battlefield, southern foundries, especially during the war's first years, would bear the brunt of supplying Confederate troops in the field.

At the same time, the U.S. Army started acquiring rifled field pieces, which fired projectiles almost the same weight as the Napoleon, but with much more accuracy than the smoothbore tubes used until then. Given the might of the relatively industrialized north, the Union Army could be relatively quickly supplied with the latest in Napoleons and iron rifled guns, including the 3-in. Ordnance Rifle and 10-pdr. Parrott gun. Except in fringe areas, such as the far western campaigns in places like New Mexico, the 6-pdr. gun was never a front-line gun in the Union forces.

The result, at the battle of Shiloh for example, was that 80 percent of the Confederate artillery was made up of 6-pdr. and 12-pdr. howitzers, while almost half the opposing artillery was modern, rifled 3-in. and 10-pdr. weapons. The 6-pdrs. were vastly outclassed: "Six-pdr. guns cannot maintain a fight with long range guns," one Confederate artilleryman wrote after the battle of Murfreesboro. At Chickamauga, the Confederate ordnance chief reported all his 6-pdrs. had been "repulsed by 12-pounder light guns." At Antietam in September, 1862, although desperately short of guns to stop Union attacks, 6-pdr. batteries such as Huckstep's 1st Fluvanna Artillery were sent to quiet places in the rear to guard fords rather than face sure defeat in fights against Union artillery.

In March, 1862, the commander of the Confederate Army of Tennessee

A U.S. Army gun crew stands in the position of "action front" with a 12-pdr. Napoleon in a fort near Atlanta, Georgia, in 1864. From this position they could either begin firing or hitch up the cannon for movement. (Library of Congress)

ordered that all the 6-pdrs. in this force be sent back to foundries and recast as light 12-pounders. Army of Northern Virginia commander Robert E. Lee recommended that all his army's 6-pdrs. be melted down and made into 12-pdrs. in December, 1862. In July, 1862, the Confederate Ordnance Department ordered the main southern gun foundry, Tredegar Iron Works in Richmond, to cease production of 6-pdrs. and start making nothing but 12-pdr. Napoleons. By mid-1863 the 6-pdr. was effectively out of service in the main theaters of action, beginning with the Army of Northern Virginia and spreading thereafter to other forces in the field.

ORGANIZATION OF THE U.S. ARMY FIELD ARTILLERY

At the start of the war it was felt that the effort to put down the rebellion would be a short one, requiring only three months' worth of service. Since training skilled artillerymen would take longer than that, initially only Regular Army artillery was to be recruited.

"The artillery of the U.S. Army is by far its worst or most slipshod organization of any branch of the service," wrote professional artilleryman Maj. Thomas Osborn in 1864. "This arm has in the regular army always been considered the aristocratic one and sought for assignments by the old officers, yet from the beginning of the war it has been permitted to remain without an organization of its own, except such as it has received as a result of incessant begging and intercession by its officers for a recognized position."

Organization in the Army of the Potomac

At first U.S. batteries were assigned one to each infantry brigade. But fairly quickly after hostilities started some far-sighted artillerymen saw that massed guns were important for battlefield success, and this required organization beyond a battery level. After Bull Run, William F. Barry, who started the war as a captain in the 2d U.S. Artillery Regiment

Once war became static in the trenches around Petersburg in 1864, even field artillery was heavily dug in. This weapon is being aimed by a gunner, while No. three stands ready at the trail to move it as indicated. Note the woven rope shield hanging in front of the gun.

and was one of the board of three who produced the standard manual for U.S. artillery during the war, suggested to George B. McClellan, the commander of the Army of the Potomac, that there were basic principles in successful artillery organization. Among these were:

"1. There should be at least two and one-half and preferably three pieces for every 1,000 men.

2. Materiel should be restricted to the system of the U.S. Ordnance Department [3-in. rifles], of Parrott's, and of smoothbores, the latter to be exclusively the 12-pounder, model 1857, variously called the 'gun-howitzer,' the 'light 12-pounder,' or the 'Napoleon.' A limited number of smoothbore howitzers would be authorized for special service.

3. Each field battery should, if practicable, be composed of six guns, never less than four, all to be of uniform caliber.

4. Field batteries would be assigned to divisions in lieu of brigades – four per division. One of the four batteries was to be a battery of Regulars, whose captain would also be the division chief-of-artillery. If divisions were combined into corps, at least one-half the division artillery was to constitute the reserve artillery of the corps.

5. There would be an artillery reserve for the whole army of 100 guns. This reserve would contain light field batteries, all guns of position, and all horse artillery until such time as the cavalry units were organized into major-size units.

6. The amount of ammunition to accompany the field batteries would not be less than 400 rounds per gun."

McClellan adopted these ideas, organizing his artillery quite some time before the Confederates. Indeed, this organization served the Army of the Potomac until May 16, 1864, when the high command of the army ordered that each six-gun battery was to be reduced to two sections of four guns, spare guns going back to Washington, and the Artillery Reserve being officially disbanded. Its batteries were reassigned to the brigade of the three infantry corps then serving in the army. This resulted in an artillery force of some 12 batteries of 48 guns with each brigade.

In March, 1865, the Army of the Potomac's artillery was again reorganized, with only six batteries being assigned to the II and VI Corps, and five batteries each to the V and IX Corps. All other batteries were reassigned to a renewed Artillery Reserve, grouped around the heavy siege guns and mortars that had joined the army for the siege of Petersburg.

A well used 20-pdr. Parrott rifle, manned by the 1st New York Battery near Richmond in June, 1862. (Library of Congress)

Organization of the Western Armies

The Army of the Cumberland arranged its artillery with three or four batteries being assigned to each division, under a chief of artillery who was usually a captain. The army itself was divided, at the battle of Stone's River, into a right wing, center, and left wing, each with a chief of artillery who was a captain. One battery, the Chicago Board of Trade battery, was posted with the Pioneer Brigade, while another was assigned to the cavalry division.

In September, 1864, Maj. Thomas Osborn, newly assigned army chief of artillery of the Army of the Tennessee, found this type of arrangement, which was used in his new command, lacking: "Since I came to this army I have made a complete reevaluation in the artillery organization of this Army and Department," he wrote. "I found its organization bad, or more exactly I found it without organization. What I have done has been against the wishes of the division and corps commanders. The several batteries were attached to the division, two or three to each division. A division chief of artillery was attached to the staff of the division commander. The returns and reports of the several batteries were generally made to the adjutant general of the division and were returned to the corps and army head-quarters as part of the division returns. The chief of artillery of the division seldom took further interest in the batteries than to keep a personal watch over them. He maintained no independent office. Naturally the division commanders desired to retain the command and control of these batteries and from long usage the corps commanders rather favored this plan. I determined to make the change and brigade the artillery of each corps of this army, as it was in the Army of the Potomac and as had been brought to the Army of the Cumberland by the XI and XII Corps and as now exists in the XX Corps composed of the consolidated XI and XII Corps." Osborn got his way.

Battery A, 2d U.S. Artillery, taken in 1862 near Fair Oaks, Virginia, was armed with 3-in. Ordnance Rifles. (Library of Congress)

The Army of the Ohio, too, used batteries assigned to brigades until Maj. Gen. George Thomas assumed command in October, 1863. Thomas assigned 18 batteries to the army's divisions, while another dozen batteries went into a general army reserve. The six Regular Army batteries with that army were posted to the reserve.

ORGANIZATION OF CONFEDERATE FIELD ARTILLERY

On November 1, 1862, the Confederate Adjutant and Inspector General's Office issued its General Orders, No. 81, which spelled out the organization of the light artillery:

"II. The following will be the organization of a company of light artillery, according to the number of guns composing the battery, viz.:

For a battery of six guns: one captain, 2 first lieutenants, 2 second lieutenants, 1 sergeant-major or first sergeant, 1 quartermaster-sergeant, 6 sergeants, 12 corporals, 2 buglers or trumpeters, 1 guidon, 2 artificers, 64 to 125 privates.

For a battery of four guns: one captain, 1 first lieutenant, 2 second lieutenants, 1 sergeant-major or first sergeant, 1 quartermaster-sergeant, 4 sergeants, 8 corporals, 2 buglers, 1 guidon, 2 artificers, 64 to 125 privates."

Eye-witness Edwin Forbes drew this battery of 3-in. Ordnance Rifles being taken into action.

These batteries were to be the basic artillery organization; banding them together to form regiments or battalions was not considered, although field-grade artillery officers were authorized.

The Army of Northern Virginia
On May 7, 1861, Virginia authorized its inspector-general to raise six batteries of four guns each for its forces. This made up the nucleus of what would become the field artillery of the Army of Northern Virginia. Following standard prewar practice, each battery was assigned under the command of an infantry brigade commander. Some leading officers

pressed for the formation of battalions as early as the winter of 1861/62, but this proposal was shelved for the time being. Confederate artillery officer E. Porter Alexander, writing of the Peninsular Campaign of 1862, said: "Our artillery, too, was even in worse need of reorganization. A battery was attached, or supposed to be, to every brigade of infantry. Beside these, a few batteries were held in reserve under old [Brigadier] Gen. [William] Pendleton [the army's chief of artillery]. Naturally our guns and ammunition were far inferior to the enemy's, & this scattering of the commands made it impossible ever to mass our guns in effective numbers. For artillery loses its effect if scattered."

Soldiers learned after a couple of years of war to dig in whenever they halted for any time at all. The men of Stevens' Battery at Cold Harbor are not only dug in, but the cannoneers duck even while going through their gun drill.

Finally, in January, 1862, Pendleton "respectfully proposed that in each corps the artillery be arranged into battalions, to consist for the most part of four batteries each, a particular battalion ordinarily to attend to a certain division, and to report to, and receive orders from, its commander, though liable to be divided, detached, etc., as the commanding general or corps commanders may seem best, past associations to be so consulted in the constitution of these batteries as that each shall, as far as practicable, contain batteries that have served together, and with the divisions which the battalion is still ordinarily to attend. These battalions ought to have, it is believed, two field officers each, a surgeon, an ordnance officer, and a bonded officer for supplies, if not both quartermaster and commissary."

This suggestion was accepted and by the start of the Chancellorsville campaign artillery battalions were generally accepted as commands independent from the infantry. A visiting Austrian officer, FitzGerald Ross, later described the organization as he viewed it in the spring of 1863: "The artillery is organized into battalions; five battalions in a corps of three divisions, one to each division, and two in reserve. They always mass the artillery now, and commanders of battalions say that they loose no more men in a battalion then they formerly did in a single battery. Each battalion is complete in itself, with quartermaster, adjutant, ordnance officer, surgeon, &c. The whole is under the control of the chief of artillery of the army, but assigned at convenience to the corps commanders, one of whose staff-officers is chief of artillery to the corps, and another chief of ordnance."

The Army of Tennessee

In 1861 the State of Tennessee adopted the standard U.S. Army field organization for its batteries, meaning each one was to have six guns and from 94 to 155 men, all ranks. This formed the standard for what became the Army of Tennessee, one of the two main field armies of the

A battery, or traveling forge, parked among the guns of a New York battery.
(Library of Congress)

Confederacy. Each battery was assigned to serve an infantry brigade, rather than having the batteries massed into battalions.

In March, 1862, Gen. P. G. T. Beauregard, commanding the Army of Tennessee, ordered the corps of Lt. Gen. Leonidas Polk, newly arrived with the rest of the army in Corinth, Mississippi, to standardize its artillery at three guns per 1,000 infantry, with uniform calibers in each battery, which were to consist of four or six guns each. In May, 1862, following the battle of Shiloh, Beauregard reduced each six-gun battery to four, with excess lieutenants being posted to heavy artillery or held to replace expected casualties.

Finally, in March, 1864, newly arrived Gen. Joseph E. Johnston organized his field artillery batteries into regular battalions, each to consist of three four-gun batteries. A major, assisted by a quartermaster, a commissary, two or three surgeons, and an adjutant, commanded each battalion. Three battalions were held as an army reserve, while each of the other battalions was assigned to a division. The three reserve battalions made up one regiment, while each corps had an artillery regiment made up of the battalions assigned to the divisions within that corps. The first regiment had 12 batteries, 48 guns, 742 horses, and 1,243 men; the second regiment had nine batteries, 36 guns, 582 horses, and 1,078 men; the third regiment had nine batteries, 36 guns, 566 horses, and 1,016 men. The battalion of horse artillery had five batteries, 22 guns, some 335 horses, and 420 men.

On 14 November 1864, Lt. Gen. John B. Hood, who replaced Johnston, (much to the chagrin of the army) reorganized the artillery, reverting to the old division-level assignments with each battalion being assigned to a particular division. This reorganization would prevent the massing of guns on a full regimental level, but in practice most battalion commanders continued to report directly to their divisional commanders, rather than the regimental commanders. It merely confirmed what had already been taking place.

EQUIPMENT

According to the basic Federal artillery manual, each gun crew should have two sponges and rammers, two sponge covers, one worm and staff, two handspikes, one sponge bucket, one prolonge (a long line used to pull a gun to the rear without horses), one tar bucket, two leather water buckets, two gunner's haversacks, two tube pouches, one fuze gouge, one fuze wrench, one vent punch, one gunner's pincers, one tow hook, one pendulum hausse (essentially a gun's detachable rear sight), two thumbstalls, one priming wire, two lanyards, one gunner's gimlet, and one large tarpaulin. Each caisson should be equipped with a felling ax, a long handled shovel, a pickax, a spare handspike, a spare pole, a spare wheel, a fuze gouge, two tow hooks, a tar bucket, two leather watering buckets, and a large tarpaulin.

Confederates captured two James rifles from the 1st Connecticut Light Battery near Charleston and, as typical of all armies, the commanding officer

A well used battery forge. (Library of Congress)

had to list every item lost to the enemy. His list gives a good idea of the essential equipment each gun crew actually brought to the field: "2 6-Pdr. James Rifles -3.80"; 2 6-Pdr. carriages with limber chests; 4 sponges & rammers; 3 sponge covers; 1 worm & staff; 4 handspikes; 2 vent covers; 2 sponge buckets, tin; 2 prolongs; 2 gunners pincers; 3 tow hooks; 1 thumbstall [one cannoneer obviously escaped]; 2 priming wires; 1 lanyards; 2 gunners gimlets; 2 fuze reamers; 2 fuze shears; 2 tompions; 1 tar bucket, tin; 2 watering buckets, leather; 1 set harness for two lead horses." Listed, but not mentioned in the official list, were the leather vent covers that were strapped around the tube to protect the weapon when not in use it, and a tompion to fit into each bore as further protection.

The same organization further listed equipment that had become unserviceable and its list indicates how long such equipment could be expected to last in the field. An iron tar bucket, a lanyard, and a sponge and rammer lasted 28 months; a sponge cover was worn out in ten months; three rammer heads were worn out in 11 months; while 6 woolen sponges were worn out in four months.

Each field battery was also supplied with a traveling forge, complete with tools and materials required for shoeing horses and doing other necessary repairs, and a battery wagon on which a variety of carpenter's and saddler's tools were stored.

AMMUNITION

"There are four kinds of projectiles used in field service," wrote the authors of the standard U.S. Army artillery field manual, "the solid shot, the canister, the shell, and the case shot.

"The projectile is attached to a block of wood called a sabot. For the guns and the 12-pdr. howitzer, the cartridge and the projectile are attached to the same sabot, making together a round of fixed ammunition ...

"The solid shot is spherical, and its weight in pounds is used to designate the caliber of the gun to which it belongs.

"The canister consists of a tin cylinder, attached to a sabot and filled with cast-iron shot. These shot vary in diameter, and of course in weight, with the caliber and description of the piece. Canisters for guns contain 27 shots each; those for howitzers contain 48 shots each. They are packed in sawdust in four tiers; the lower tier rests on a rolled iron plate, which is placed on the sabot, and the canister is closed with a sheet-iron cover ...

"The shell is a hollow shot, with such thickness of metal as enables it to penetrate earthworks, wooden buildings, &c., without breaking. For service it is charged with powder, and bursts with great force. Firing is communicated to the charge by means of a fuze, inserted in the hole through which the powder is introduced, the time of the explosion being regulated by the preparation of the fuze. The shell is designated by the weight of the solid shot of the same diameter.

"The shrapnel or case shot is a hollow cast-iron shot forming a case which is filled with musket balls. Melted sulphur or resin is poured in to fill up the interstices and secure the balls in their positions. After this is solidified, a portion of the contents is bored out and the vacant cylindrical space filled with powder, the amount of the charge being only sufficient to rupture the case, which has less thickness of metal than the shell, and to disperse the contents. Fire is communicated to the charge by the means employed for exploding the shell."

While both sides used the same types of ammunition, southern-made rounds were noticeably poorer in quality than northern-made ones. E. Porter Alexander, a Confederate artillery battalion commander, commented that in 1861: "Our smooth bore shells & shrapnel would

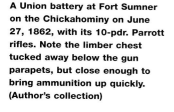

A Union battery at Fort Sumner on the Chickahominy on June 27, 1862, with its 10-pdr. Parrott rifles. Note the limber chest tucked away below the gun parapets, but close enough to bring ammunition up quickly. (Author's collection)

very frequently explode prematurely, & our rifle shot & shells would all tumble or fail to go point first, so they had no range at all & were worse than worthless ... We gradually made great improvements, but the enemy were always far ahead of us in artillery ammunition of all kinds both in quality & quantity."

A flannel bag containing the powder was inserted separately from each round of ammunition.

Gun	Item	Number of rounds (U.S.)	Weight in pounds (U.S.)	Number of rounds (CS)	Weight in pounds (CS)
6-lb.	Shot	25	190	25	190
	Spherical case	20	140	20	140
	Canister	5	42	5	42
Total rounds		50		50	
	Spare 1.4-lb. cartridges	2	2.5	2	2.6
	Primers	75	.6	75	.97
	Yds. slow match	1.5	.4	2	.38
	Port-fires	3	.6	2	.57
Total Weight			376.1 lb.		376.52 lb.
12-lb.	Shot	20	308	12	184.8
	Spherical case	8	117.6	12	176.4
	Shell	0	0	4	48.68
	Canister	4	67.6	4	67.64
Total rounds		32		32	
	Spare 2.5-lb. cartridges	2	5	2	5.12
	Primers	48	.4	48	.62
	Yds. slow match	2	.5	1.5	.28
	Port-fires	4	.7	3	.57
Total Weight			499.8 lb.		484.11 lb.
12-lb. howitzer	Shell	15	157.5	15	157.5
	Spherical case	20	273	20	273
	Canister	4	47.4	4	47.4
Total rounds		39		39	
	Primers	6	.5	58	47.4
	Yds. slow match	1.5	.4	2	.38
	Port-fires	3	.6	3	.57
Total Weight			479.4 lb.		479.6 lb.

FUSES

The Bormann fuse, a circular metal disk about an inch-and-a-half in diameter and a half-inch thick was most commonly used. It was tapped so it could be screwed into the shell, while the inside was filled with a

A close-up of a limber chest on a limber. Note the foot boards used by cannoneers for riding. (George Lomas Collection)

circular train of powder. Its face was marked with a set of parallel lines of differing lengths and numbers, each representing a different time. The gunner cut into the fuse at the proper point for the shell to explode at a given time. The first mark exploded the shell at three quarters of a second after firing; the second, one second; the third, a second and a quarter; the fourth, a second and a half; the fifth, a second and three quarters; the sixth, a number 2, at two seconds; and so fourth up to five and a quarter seconds. This proved to be the most reliable fuse in Federal service.

The poor quality of southern-made Bormann fuses caused battery commanders some problems. According to Alexander: "Confederate artillery could only sparingly, & in great emergency, be allowed to fire over the heads of our infantry. We were always liable to premature explosions of shell & shrapnel, & our infantry knew it by sad experience, & I have known of their threatening to fire back at our guns if we opened over their heads. Of course, solid shot could be safely so used, but that is the least effective ammunition, & the infantry would not know the difference & would be demoralized & angry all the same." Indeed, production of southern-made Bormann fuses was discontinued in December, 1862, although some batteries were forced to use them as late as Gettysburg. Instead, the Confederates used a variety of fuses, ranging from simple paper models to an elaborate device that used a bullet attached to a friction primer. As the shell rotated in the barrel, the bullet was spun off, igniting the primer which had been previously picked for the correct time required.

The Federal artillery also experimented with placing a percussion cap on a cone under a metal cover on the nose of ammunition fired with rifled guns. Since the nose of a round fired with a rifled gun would hit the target first, the percussion cap would then fire the shell on impact. This meant that estimating times for setting fuses would be unnecessary. The Confederates used similar fuses made of copper which screwed into the shell nose.

Due to the problems of premature explosions when firing over infantry, J. P. Shenkl produced a 3-in. Ordnance Rifle shell encased in papier-mâché which would turn into harmless powder as it flew towards its target. Another maker, James, produced ammunition for his system of rifled smoothbores that used a long soft-metal covering that fit into the grooves on firing. The cast-iron body was oblong and had a cast of slanted iron ribs under the tinplate and lead covering. The special ammunition produced by Wiard for his guns used a cast-iron body loaded with shot and bound by wire. The wire was connected to projections at the end. Small holes allowed the gas on discharge to enter the projectile, expanding its sides.

THE M1857 NAPOLEON

The first Napoleon was cast in December, 1856, by the Ames Manufacturing Co., Chicopee, Massachusetts. It was the only exact copy of the French Army's field piece, complete with handles on the top above the trunnions, and a full 61-in. long tube. There was some dissatisfaction with the results obtained with this length barrel, and future tubes were made some three inches longer. The original tube is presently located at the Petersburg (Virginia) National Military Park.

Ames cast four more tubes in 1857, followed by another four in February, 1861. All of these guns were the same as the first, save for the added three inches to the tube. This was the total complement of Napoleons when the Civil War broke out.

They proved highly successful. A Napoleon could fire a 2.5 lb. charge, sending solid shot some 1,680 yards, a range that easily encompassed the major battlefields of the period. Its crews could fire solid shot, spherical case, and shell, not to mention canister, which against personnel at ranges of some 300 yards was amazingly deadly. Moreover, it was a dependable weapon. George D. Ramsay, then a brigadier general and Chief of Ordnance, reported in July, 1864, that: "No instance has occurred during the war ... of the 12-pdr. bronze gun (the Napoleon) having worn out or of its bursting ..."

Although the army had been using a version of the Napoleon for almost four years when the war broke out, its ordnance officials wanted to compare it against the French models. Therefore, in June, 1861, the Secretary of War requested "from France a sample of Napoleon gun, or one of each caliber, both rifled and smooth bored, if there be more than one caliber and kind."

In August, 1861, with the army satisfied that it

This M1857 12-pdr. Napoleon was made by Ames, serial number 78, and dated 1862. (Gettysburg National Battlefield Park)

The markings on the muzzle of the M1857 12-pdr. include, clockwise from left, the weapon number, the weight of the tube, the date of manufacture, and the inspector's initials.

had a good imitation of the French cannon, Ames cast another ten Napoleons. Ames was not capable of producing all the cannon required by the U.S. Army, and contracts were granted that year to Cyrus Alger & Company (the South Boston Iron Works), which had produced cannon for the U.S. Army since 1836. Even this addition was not enough, and contracts were also given to The Revere Copper Co. and Henry N. Hooper & Co., both of Boston for yet more Napoleons. Miles Greenwood & Co., of Cincinnati, Ohio, received contracts for a limited number of Napoleons for the western theater.

These weapons were intended to bear markings as required by an 1840 Ordnance Department regulation:

"All cannon are required to be weighed and to be marked as follows, viz.: the number of the gun, and the initials of the inspector's name, on the face of the muzzle; the number in a separate series for each kind and caliber at each foundry; the initial letters of the name of the founder and of the foundry, on the end of the right trunnion; the year of fabrication on the end of the left trunnion; the foundry number on the end of the right rimbase, above the trunnion; the weight of the piece in pounds on the base of the breech; the letters 'U.S.' on the upper surface of the piece, near the end of the reinforce."

In 1861 orders were sent out for all marks, save the rimbase number and the U.S., to be placed on the muzzle face. All the 1861 Ames guns used the old marking system, but later Ames tubes used the new system. Alger changed to the new system in December, 1861, and the other makers used the new system from the beginning. Napoleons cast after the first 36 weapons had been delivered to the army were simplified by the removal of the handles, or dolphins. These began to see service by late 1861.

At least one variation to the standard bronze U.S. Army Napoleon, made without handles, should be noted. The Phoenix Iron Co., which made 3-in. Ordnance Rifles under U.S. Army contract, made what appears to be a wrought iron copy of a Napoleon, without the characteristic muzzle swell, apparently in 1863. The tube, now in the town square of Jefferson, Pennsylvania, bears markings which are standard on the company's Ordnance Rifles, although the tube weighs around 1,220 lb. rather than the 815 lb. of the Ordnance Rifles. It lacks the required initials of a U.S. Army ordnance officer, suggesting it was made as an experimental piece to test wrought iron as a substitute for bronze.

There was also an experiment to rifle the tubes. Six rifled Napoleons have survived: all are at the Gettysburg National Military Park. These were all made by Ames (numbers 77 to 82) and used a rifling system devised by a Charles T. James, with ten deep, narrow grooves cut into the bores of the tubes, which allowed the weapons to retain the same 4.62-in. bore diameter.

A letter from Ramsay, then a lieutenant-colonel, to Ordnance Department chief Brig. Gen. J. W. Ripley dated August 2, 1862, says that the trials of the three batteries of rifled Napoleons proved satisfactory.

Even so, the existing tubes were never stamped with an ordnance inspector's initials, nor with the "U.S." on their tops. No further James-rifled Napoleons were made. The comparatively soft bronze tubes wore out sooner than iron-rifled tubes, and if smoldering cartridge fragments settled into the grooves and were not put out by sponging, they could provoke premature discharges.

Other than these experimental weapons, Napoleons were produced throughout the war without major variations. Minor variations included two small bronze blocks cast into the tube at its breech. The pendulum hausse bracket was cast at the top of the tube's breech, and these were omitted on Greenwood tubes. The bracket at the bottom was the base plate, designed to provide a flattened surface where the tube rested on the elevating screw bore. Hooper tubes lacked the base plate. All other tubes had both.

A close-up of the James rifle, showing the novel front sight that was cast as part of the barrel. (Gettysburg Battlefield National Park)

As senior Confederate officers had almost universally been U.S. Army officers, it is not surprising that the Southern Army eventually adopted the 12-pdr. Napoleon as its standard field piece. However, the lack of manufacturing ability affected the quality and types of southern-made Napoleons. Moreover, the Confederate Army had many older weapons in its batteries, including quite a number of 6-pdrs., which came from various southern state arsenals, and did not find an immediate need to change to a new weapon.

On December 5, 1862, Robert E. Lee, commanding the Army of Northern Virginia, wrote to the Secretary of War: "I am greatly in need of longer range smooth-bore guns, and propose that, if metal cannot otherwise be procured, a portion, if not all, of our 6-pounder smooth-bores (bronze), and, if necessary, a part of our 12-pounder howitzers, be recast into 12-pounder Napoleons... The contest between our 6-pounder smooth-bores and the 12-pounder Napoleons of the enemy is very unequal, and, in addition, is discouraging to our artillerists."

Change was already underway. On November 13, 1862, the Confederate Chief of Ordnance, Col. Josiah Gorgas, issued a circular stating:

"Until further order, no artillery will be made except the following caliber:
Bronze - Light 12-pounder or Napoleon guns, caliber 4.62.
Iron - For field battery of maneuver, 10-pounder Parrotts, banded, caliber 2.9. For field battery of reserve, 20-pounder Parrotts on 12-pounder carriages, caliber 3.67. For siege guns, 30-pounder Parrotts on 18-pounder siege-carriages, caliber 4.2."

The most important supplier of southern Napoleons was J. R. Anderson & Co., better known as the Tredegar Iron Works, in Richmond, Virginia. It had experience casting cannon dating back to the 1840s, and began casting guns first for southern states and, by summer 1861, for the Confederate government itself. Unfortunately for the production of Napoleons, the south ran into a severe copper

Another view of the most common weapon of the war: the northern-made M1857 Napoleon. (Gettysburg Battlefield National Park)

A Confederate-made Napoleon 12-pdr. cannon from the Columbus, Georgia, Foundry. (Gettysburg Battlefield National Park)

shortage that by May, 1861, halted the manufacture of any bronze guns. By December, when enough copper was found, (much of which came from stills and church bells) bronze casting could resume, but the metal shortage was to plague southern gun founders throughout the war. Although copper was available from time to time, Tredegar found it difficult to get enough of the precious material to produce Napoleons in even the required numbers. By early 1863 Lee had sent his 6-pdr. tubes back to Richmond where they were made into new cannon, so that Tredegar Napoleon production began in earnest in the first half of 1863. Lee received a number just before Chancellorsville, and a second batch somewhat later. By Gettysburg he had received 49 Tredegar Napoleons, and was able to replace all the army's 6-pounders.

By July, 1863, a visiting Austrian Army officer, FitzGerald Ross, was able to record: "The field-piece most generally employed is the smooth-bored 12-pound 'Napoleon' (canon obusier), which fires solid shot, shell, case, and canister: it is much lighter than the ordinary 12-pounder, and they can give it an elevation of nine to ten degrees." Ross went on to say: "In Northern Virginia 12-pound howitzers and 6-pdr. guns are discarded, and Napoleons have been cast from their metal," adding, "for general use, almost all consider the Napoleon most serviceable."

The Tredegar Napoleons were also different from Federal Napoleons in that they lacked the muzzle swell. Some Confederate officers said the Tredegar version jarred less than northern-made weapons, but many others felt that the U.S. Army versions were superior. The majority of Tredegar Napoleons went to the Army of Northern Virginia.

The other major Confederate Army, the Army of Tennessee, originally received its Napoleons from two sources. The first, Leeds & Co., went out of production when their home city of New Orleans was captured in April, 1862; the second, Quinby & Robinson, cast guns until their home city of Memphis fell to the U.S. Navy in June, 1862, and then switched production to Cartersville, Georgia.

In March, 1863, much the same as in the east, Army of Tennessee commander Gen. Braxton Bragg ordered that his army's 6-pdrs. gradually be phased out, and recast into Napoleons. Most of this work was done in three arsenals. The Augusta Arsenal, Augusta, Georgia, cast Napoleons that differed from other southern weapons in that the junction of the barrel and breech was rounded and not sharp.

These guns were first produced in late 1862. The Augusta guns were made of a metal developed by Austrian gunsmiths which included copper, tin, wrought iron, and zinc. Each weapon was tested by loading with a charge of powder, followed by bolts rammed in clear to the muzzle.

The remaining two arsenals were the Columbus, Georgia, which was formed with equipment taken from the Baton Rouge (Louisiana) Arsenal, and began producing Napoleons in mid-1863 and the Macon, Georgia, Arsenal, which produced its first Napoleons in early 1863.

Two Napoleons cast and marked by the Charleston, South Carolina, Arsenal are known to exist today. One is dated 1863 and the other, a year later. The weapons cast in this arsenal likely saw use with forces defending the coastline. In May, 1863, Col. A. J. Gonzales, wrote to the commander of defending forces in that city that: "as soon as Napoleon guns are procured, of which four will soon be cast at the Charleston Arsenal, I will have the honor to earnestly advocate ... the formation of batteries of horse artillery, with four Napoleons each ..." All of these other southern-made Napoleons also lack the muzzle swell found in U.S. Army versions.

In November, 1863, northern forces captured the vital copper mines in Ducktown, Tennessee, something that brought an instant halt to the casting of bronze Napoleons in the south. Tredegar's experts produced an experimental version of the Napoleon made of iron, with a two-inch thick breech reinforcement added for extra strength. Heavier than the bronze model, the iron Napoleon proved serviceable. After testing in March, the Ordnance Department authorized the making of iron Napoleons with a higher priority than any other type of artillery. One Richmond Howitzers member later recalled that: "the iron gun was not only equally safe from explosion, but soon accomplished every purpose against the foe possible with the brass gun and did not create the sharp, piercing ring so severe as not infrequently caused blood to break from the ear of the cannoneer."

Despite the number of Napoleon makers in the south, the major supplier of Confederate artillery was the U.S. Army. Lt. Col. Arthur Fremantle, Coldstream Guards, visited Lee's Army of Northern Virginia in July, 1863, noting that: "The artillery. is of all kinds - Parrots [sic], Napoleons, rifled and smooth bores, all shapes and sizes. Most of them bear the letters U.S., showing that they have changed masters." Confederate artillerymen preferred to use the higher quality U.S. Army-issue weapons rather than southern-made ones. Private Joseph Garey, Hudson's Battery, recorded a typical reaction to southern-made cannon in his diary on October 17, 1861: "We received our howitzers last night. They proved of a very inferior quality, especially the wood work which is too weak to stand hard usage."

A southern-made copy of the Napoleon made by the Macon, Georgia, Arsenal in 1863. (Gettysburg National Battlefield Park)

Rear view showing the elevating screw of a Confederate Napoleon made in 1864. (Gettysburg National Battlefield Park)

THE FEDERAL NAPOLEON

Maker	Location	Number delivered
Ames Manufacturing Co.	Chicopee, MA	103
Cyrus Alger & Co.	Boston, MA	170
Henry N. Hooper & Co.	Boston, MA	370
Miles Greenwood & Co.	Cincinnati, OH	52
Revere Copper Co.	Boston, MA	461
Total		1,156

THE CONFEDERATE NAPOLEON

Maker	Location	Number Delivered
J. R. Anderson Co.*	Richmond, VA	226
Augusta Arsenal	Augusta, GA	c. 130
Charleston Arsenal	Charleston, SC	c. 20
Columbus Arsenal	Columbus, GA	52
Leeds & Co.	New Orleans, LA	12
Macon Arsenal	Macon, GA	53
Quinby & Robinson	Memphis, TN	8
Total		c. 501

*Tredegar Iron Works, cast both brass and iron

GUN RANGES

A comparison in listing of ranges from the CS Ordnance Manual, 1863, and the U.S. Instruction for Field Artillery, 1864.

Weapon	Charge (lb)	Ammunition	Elevation (degrees)	CS Range (yards)	U.S. Range (yards)
6-lb. gun	1.25	Shot	0	318	320
			1	674	675
			2	867	870
			3	1138	1140
			4	1256	1250
			5	1523	1525
12-lb. gun	2.5	Shot	0	325	350
			1	620	660
			2	875	900
			3	1200	1270
			4	1320	1450
			5	1680	1660
12-lb. howitzer	1	Shell	0	195	200
			1	539	540
			2	640	640
			3	847	840
			4	975	975
			5	1072	1070

THE 10- AND 20-PDR. PARROTT RIFLE

A West Point graduate who had resigned his commission in 1836 to head a private foundry, Robert P. Parrott developed this simple, rugged, and effective weapon. Essentially his design was a long, cast-iron tube with a wrought-iron reinforcing wedge-shaped bar wrapped around the breech, and the joints pounded together until welded shut. In the process, the tube was rotated on rollers, a stream of water being shot inside to keep the tube cool, as the hot band was wrapped around it. Because the tube rotated, the band cooled and clamped itself to the breech uniformly, instead of being tighter where the weight pulled the band down on the top of a stationary piece, while the bottom part was less tightly bound to the tube.

The band allowed the breech to absorb greater stress than an unbanded, or even typically banded cannon. Indeed, the weapon was known as a tough cannon that could take a beating and remain in use. Easy and cheap to produce, they were manufactured at the West Point Foundry under Parrott's supervision.

The Parrott was not a total success, however. In October, 1865, the Chief of Ordnance reported that: "The many failures, by bursting, of the celebrated Parrott guns in the land and naval service have weakened confidence in them, and make it the imperative duty of this department to seek elsewhere for a more reliable rifle gun." This was apt to happen after prolonged service and the weak spot was usually just ahead of the breech band. At least one 20-pdr. Parrott in Massenburg's Georgia Battery burst at its muzzle on the second day of the siege of Chattanooga, so it was not always the breech that burst. The larger weapons were, however, more liable to burst than the standard field 10-pdrs., although none could be wholly trusted.

Parrott himself addressed the problem on June 21, 1864, writing to Maj. Gen. J. G. Foster:

"Though I suppose most of the points of importance in regard to the service of my guns are by this time understood, there are one or two that are of such exceeding interest that I am induced to mention them. The greatest difficulty now to be encountered is in the premature explosion of shells in the bore of the gun. The charge of powder they will hold is quite large, and owing to the elongated form of the projectile or to its being driven into the groves, there seems to be a tendency of the parts of the broken shell to wedge in the bore, thus carrying away muzzle or some other part,

The 20-pdr. Parrott rifle could be quickly spotted in the field by its massive breech. Markings indicate that this tube weighs 1,974 pounds. (Gettysburg National Battlefield Park)

A view of a 10-pdr. Parrott rifled cannon. (Gettysburg National Battlefield Park)

or, at any rate, giving the gun a violent strain which is afterward and perhaps by other accidents developed into the destruction of the gun. As a means of diminishing this danger, I am now lacquering or varnishing the interior surface of the shells. Even when freshly put in it operates favorably. A little poured in at the fuse hole and then caused to run over the sides by laying the shells down and rolling it will answer. The reason for this seems to be that on firing the gun the powder charge of the shells is violently thrown back, and explosion is caused by the friction or attrition of the powder against the rough surface of the bottom and sides of the shell. These are made smooth by the lacquer or varnish, &c."

Nor was the distrust universal. Cannoneer John D. Billings, 10th Massachusetts Battery, recalled that in August, 1864, his battery was re-equipped with 10-pdr. Parrotts: "They were beauties and gained our regard at once," he wrote, "completely usurping the place the Rodmans [3-in. Ordnance Rifles] had held there."

The first Parrott, a so-called 10-pdr., was produced in 1860 and the weapons went into full-time production in 1861. While the 10- and 20-pdrs. were the standard field piece, Parrott also built 30-, 100-, 200-, 300-, and even a 600-pdr. version of the same weapon. The first version of the 10-pdr. weapon had a 2.9-in. bore with three lands and groves of around the same size. This version was marked by a slight muzzle swell. In 1863 a newer version, one that remained standard throughout the war, appeared with a 3-in. bore, three lands and groves, and no muzzle swell. The U.S.-issue weapons are marked with a date and the initials "RPP" and "WPF".

This 10-pdr. Parrott rifle was made in 1863. (Gettysburg National Battlefield Park)

The 20-pdr. had a 3.67-in. bore with five lands and groves. They were marked "20-Pdr." on the left trunnion, although their massive breeches made them clearly identifiable in any gun park. One period expert noted that: "The 20-pdr. Parrott ... proved to be too small to give the precision of fire demanded of a siege gun and to be too heavy for convenient use as a field gun. Moreover, its projectiles did not seem to take the grooves as well as those of either smaller or larger calibers. The gun was accordingly not regarded with favor." Indeed, after Antietam, most of the 20-pdrs. in the Army of the Potomac were replaced with 10-pdr. Parrotts or 3-in. Ordnance Rifles.

In 1862 alone, the army bought 344 Parrott guns of various sizes. Indeed, by that year's end, the army had purchased 411 Parrott field guns, 108 siege guns, and 38 sea coast defense guns. The Parrott, then, was among the most common of all Union field pieces, despite its problems.

This Southern-made copy of the 10-pdr. Parrott rifle bears the serial number 4 on the muzzle. (Gettysburg National Battlefield Park)

The ease of making such cannon did not escape the Confederates, and J. R. Anderson & Co. cast copies at its Tredegar Iron Works in Richmond beginning in November, 1861. The first ones cast were 6-pdr. versions of the weapon, a bore size they continued to produce until August, 1862. In July they cast their first 30-pdr. Parrott copy, followed by a 10-pdr. in August. All told, by the war's end the works had produced some 58 copies of the 10-pdr. Parrott rifle and 45 copies of the 20-pdr. largely for use in the Army of Northern Virginia.

Starting in August, 1863, the Macon Arsenal made around a dozen copies of the 10-pdr. Parrott mostly for the Army of Mississippi. The Arsenal also cast some 20- and 30-pdr. Parrotts as well. The chief of artillery for the Army of Tennessee, which received a battery of Macon's 10-pdrs. tested these southern-made weapons and found the results were: "so much unsatisfactory that I really do not understand its cause." Rifling was found to be uneven and bore diameter was not uniform. A handful of Parrott copies may also have been produced at the Augusta, Georgia, Arsenal also for the Army of Tennessee use. A private company, Street, Hungerford & Co., Memphis, Tennessee, made at least three, and possibly more, copies of the Parrott gun. Finally, Bujac & Bennett, New Orleans, produced a dozen copies of the Parrott rifle in December, 1861, of which three burst immediately, followed by another eight in March, 1862.

This six-foot-tall man demonstrates the size of the 10-pdr. Parrott rifle. (Gettysburg Battlefield National Park)

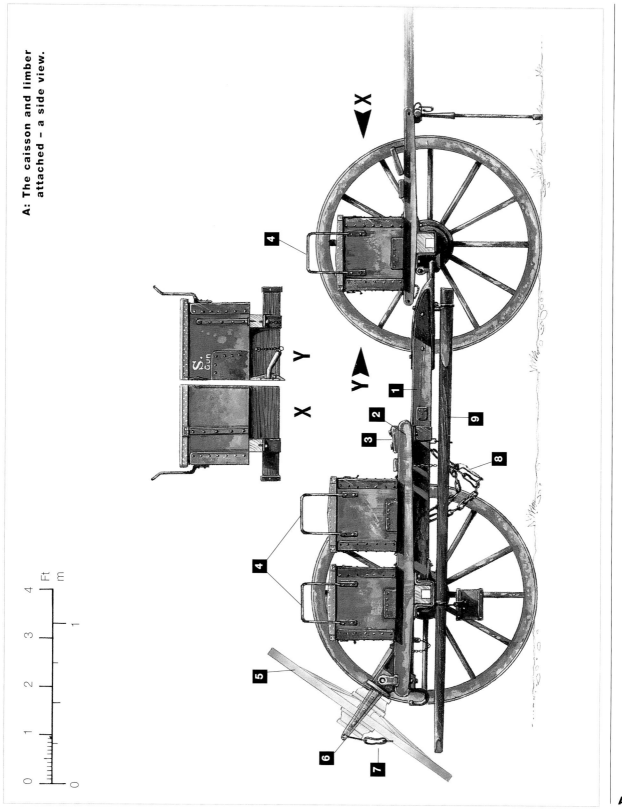

A: The caisson and limber attached – a side view.

Ft
m

4 3 2 1 0

X Y

A

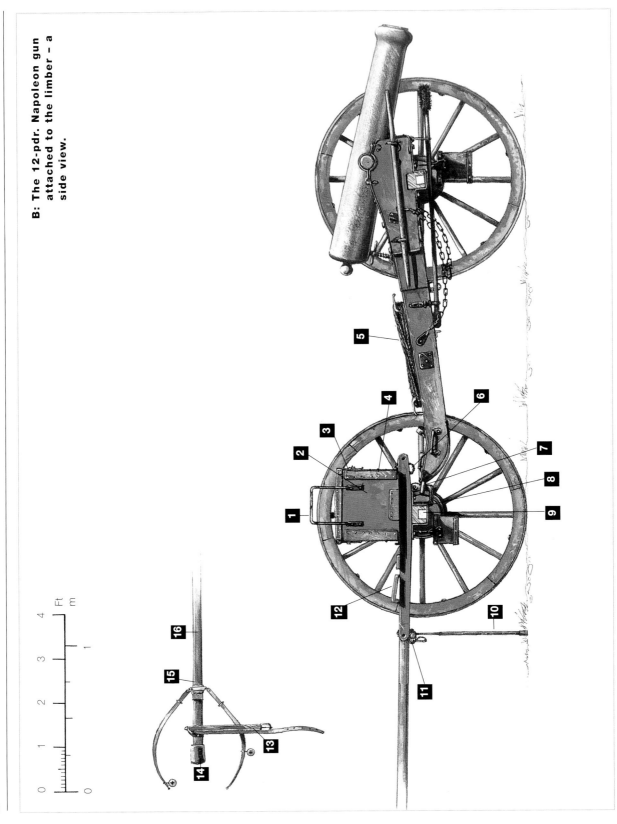

B: The 12-pdr. Napoleon gun attached to the limber – a side view.

B

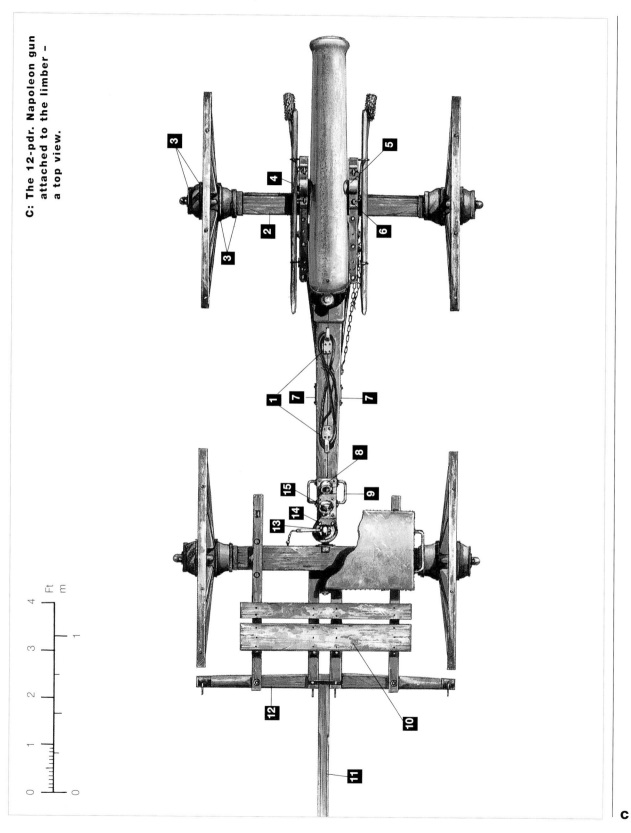

C: The 12-pdr. Napoleon gun attached to the limber – a top view.

C

6-PDR FIELD GUN CARRIAGE

12-pdr. Howitzer

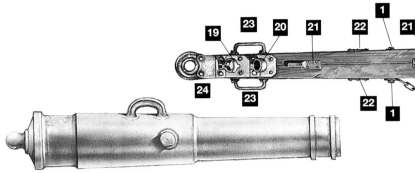

24-pdr. Howitzer

6-pdr. Gun

3-in. Ordnance Rifle

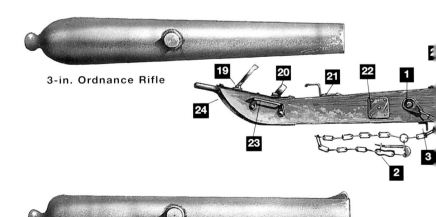

10-pdr. James Rifle

D

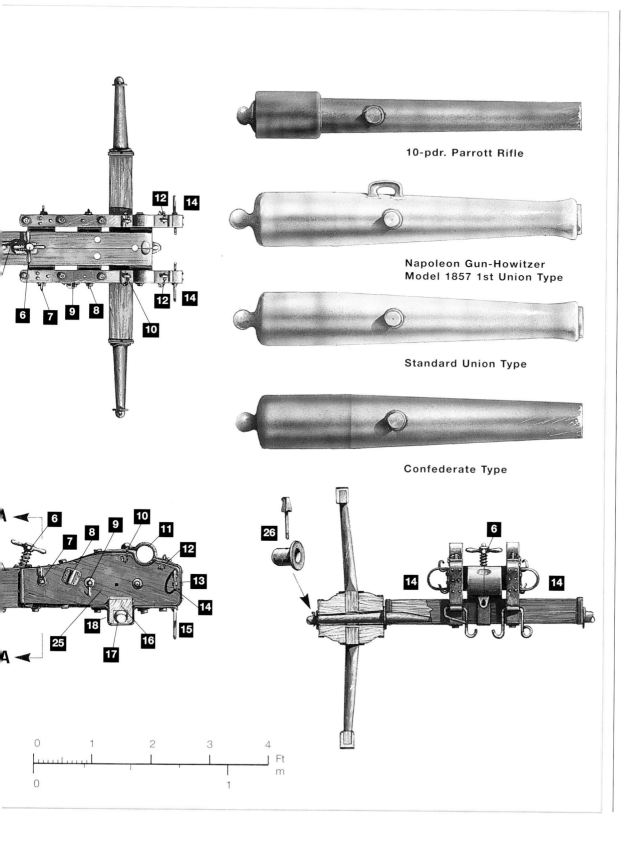

10-pdr. Parrott Rifle

Napoleon Gun-Howitzer
Model 1857 1st Union Type

Standard Union Type

Confederate Type

Ft
m

E: A battery wagon.
Top and side views
with a cutaway of the
interior from the top.

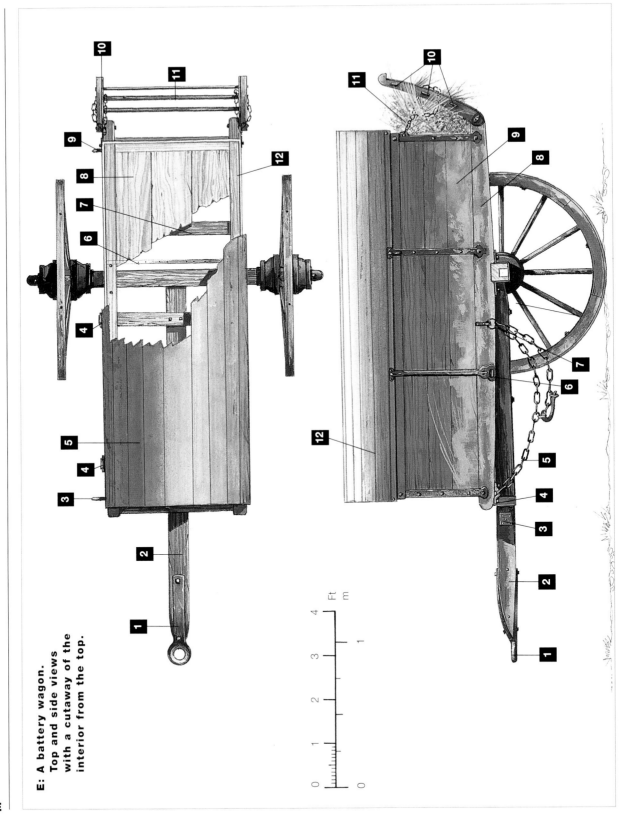

E

F: The traveling forge – top and side cutaway views.

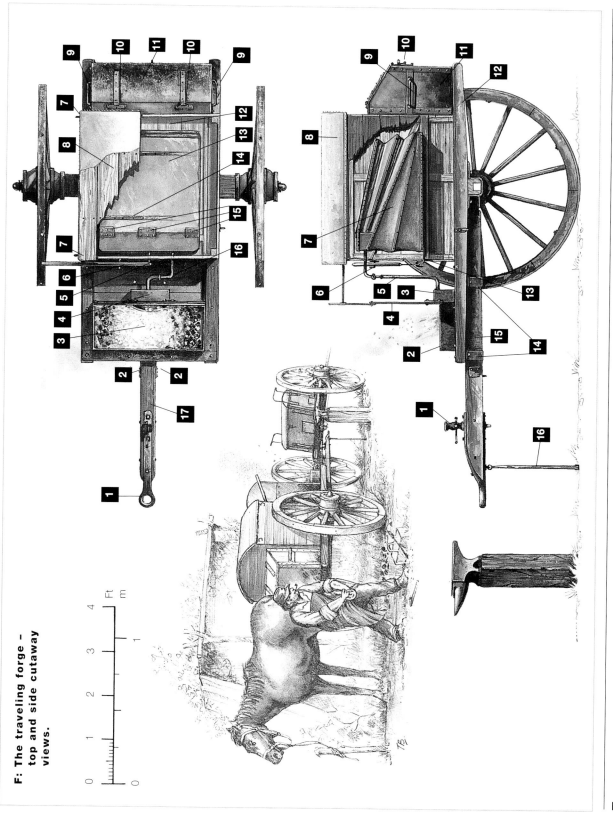

F

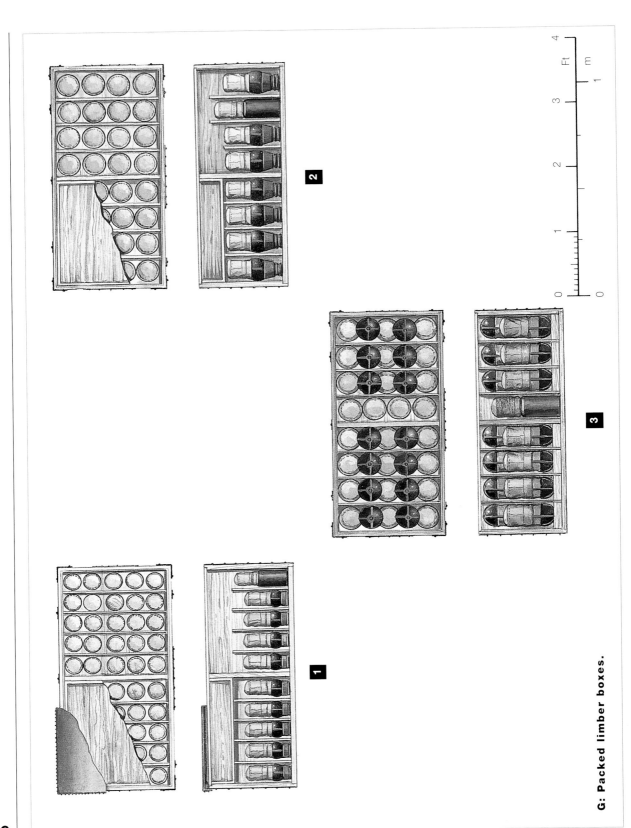

G: Packed limber boxes.

THE 3-IN. ORDNANCE RIFLE

A private citizen, John Griffen, superintendent of the Phoenix Iron Co., Phoenixville, Pennsylvania, developed a system of making artillery in the 1850s that proved highly successful. His foundry took strips of wrought iron some 3/4 of an inch wide and 4.5 inches thick and wrapped them by lathe around an iron core. In all, five layers were built around the core with a thin iron covering on top. Then the core was removed and a plug driven into the breech which not only closed the breech, but also formed the cascabel. Then the mass was heated to welding temperature and up-set two inches in a press. It was rolled out from 4.5 to 7 feet and the bore was reamed out. Trunnions were welded on and the chase turned down to a proper size in a lathe.

The end result was a 3-in. rifled weapon with clean lines and light weight. It was made with 0.5-in.-wide lands and grooves that were 0.84 inches wide. The standard tube weight was 820 lb., although many were slightly lighter. Tests made during the war with a pound of powder and a 9-lb. shell at 10 degrees showed a range of 2,788 yards, while a 20 degree elevation gave the weapon a range of 3,972 yards. It was also an exceptionally safe weapon: only one 3-in. rifle was recorded as having burst in the Union Army during the entire war.

It passed government tests and on June 25, 1861, the Ordnance Department ordered 200 rifled versions of this weapon, and another 100 smoothbores. In fact, the order was quickly changed to make all 300 weapons rifles, and eventually the Phoenix Iron Co. supplied the U.S. Army with 1,100 weapons by the war's end. Each is marked on its muzzle with the inspector's initials, the weapon serial number, the weight, "PICo," and the date of manufacture. They were called both Ordnance Rifles and 3-in. Rifles by their users.

These weapons were popular with users on both sides. Brig. Gen. George D. Ramsay, Chief of Ordnance, reported`that: "The experience of wrought iron field guns is most favorable to their endurance and efficiency. They cost less than steel and stand all the charge we want to impose on them ..." Confederate artilleryman E. Porter Alexander referred to "the beautiful United States Three-Inch Ordnance Rifles." And Confederate Army Headquarters reported at the end of 1861 that, "The outstanding orders for artillery embrace 15 15-inch columbiads, 220 10-inch columbiads, 340 8-inch columbiads, 70 8-inch siege howitzers, 158 3-inch rifle guns, 24 12-pdr. howitzers, 40 24-pdr. howitzers, 20 10-in. howitzers, 80 42- pounder siege guns, 100 32-pounder siege guns, and field batteries to the extent of our necessities."

A 3-in. Ordnance Rifle made in 1863. (Gettysburg National Battlefield Park)

While some Confederate batteries received 3-in. rifles on their foundation, many weapons became southern property through prewar purchases and captures. It was not until January, 1862, that the Tredegar Iron Works cast its first 3-in. rifle, and it produced a total of only 20, none of them after April, 1862. Noble Brothers & Co., Rome, Georgia, a private contractors, started manufacturing 3-in. rifles in 1861, producing

18 of them for both Richmond and Augusta Arsenals between April, 1861, and October, 1862, when they ceased production.

Quinby & Robinson, of Memphis, Tennessee, another private concern, produced four versions of the 3-in. rifle using bronze as the barrel metal between November, 1861, and June, 1862, when the city was captured by Federal forces. Bronze was also used as the barrel metal for the three 3-in. rifles produced in 1862 by A. B. Reading & Brother, Vicksburg, Mississippi, which saw use in the Army of Mississippi. The Bellona Foundry also cast some bronze and iron 3-in. rifles, known in the Confederate service as "Burton and Archers," but these were especially prone to bursting. The term "Burton and Archer" came from the special ammunition designed for these weapons.

Muzzle of the first 3-inch Ordnance Rifle ever produced. This particular weapon was captured at Gettysburg. (George Lomas Collection)

THE M1841 12-PDR. HOWITZER

The smoothbore howitzer was designed as a lightweight gun suitable for use with canister or shell at short ranges, or at a higher trajectory than regular guns; it was therefore able to hit targets in greater defilade than regular guns. The Model 1841 12-pdr. howitzer, with its bronze 65 in.-long tube that weighed 788 lb., fired an 8.9 lb. shell 1,072 yards at five degrees elevation with a one-pound charge of powder. The weapon was not popular with artillerymen who were forced to engage in counter-battery fire against superior Napoleons, 3-in. rifles, and Parrott guns.

In March, 1864, Army of Northern Virginia chief William Pendleton inspected the artillery of the Army of Tennessee and reported that 12-pdr. howitzers were "scarcely more valuable" than 6-pdr. smoothbores, which he called "nearly useless, if not indeed worse." At that time about a quarter of the army's artillery park consisted of 12-pdr. howitzers. Pendleton felt that the howitzers were useful only in broken

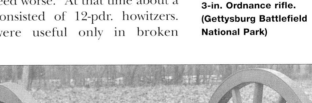

Another view of the 3-in. Ordnance rifle. (Gettysburg Battlefield National Park)

wooded country, and therefore called for the replacement of many of the weapons then in use. Lee agreed, suggesting that they be melted down to make new Napoleons. Nonetheless, many remained in the Confederate service until the war's end, and E. Porter Alexander mentioned rigging up his howitzers on skids, aimed at high elevations, to use them successfully as mortars.

The howitzer was also useful in close defense. Writing about artillery in

A 12-pdr. Confederate-made howitzer. (Gettysburg National Battlefield Park)

The Ordnance Manual drawing of the 12-pdr. mountain howitzer on its carriage as well as the pack saddle used to carry the tube shown on the first horse, and the two limber chests on the second horse.

the Petersburg campaign, Union artillery general Henry Abbot claimed that in being attacked: "no artillery can be more efficient than the 32-pdr. or 24-pdr. field howitzer." He went on to mention being attacked at a post held by a company of the 1st Connecticut Heavy Artillery, armed with two 32-pdr. and one 24-pdr. howitzers in which "so rapid a canister fire was maintained as to repulse the column with severe loss."

The Confederates developed the Model 1862 12-pdr. field howitzer which had an iron 64.4 in.-long tube with a bore of 4.62 inches and a weight of 850 pounds. They actually first cast these at the Tredegar Iron Works in November, 1861, and later began casting bronze 12-pounders, too. In all, the Tredegar Iron Works cast some 30 iron versions, none after June, 1862, and 34 bronze versions, none after November, 1862.

Some private southern concerns also cast 12-pdr. howitzers, among them T. M. Brennan & Co., of Nashville, Tennessee, which cast 20 of them before the foundry was captured. In Memphis, Tennessee, Quinby & Robinson turned out 43 12-pdr. howitzers, the last three of which were unfinished when the factory burned down, ending production. John Clark & Co., of New Orleans, cast a number used in western armies before that city's fall. Another New Orleans firm, Leeds & Co., produced nine 12-pdr. howitzers in the same period. The Columbus (Georgia) Iron Works cast at least a couple of brass howitzers, one made from household brass items donated by local ladies. Noble Brothers & Co., Rome, Georgia, turned out 14 12-pdr. howitzers in 1861–62. A. B. Reading & Brother, Vicksburg, Mississippi, delivered a pair of 12-pdr.

A captured Confederate 12-pdr. howitzer complete with limber. (Library of Congress)

howitzers in 1861–62. Washington Foundry, Richmond, produced ten bronze rough-finished 12-pdr. howitzers in 1862 that were finished in the Richmond machine shop of Samson & Pac.

As indicated by Abbot, the howitzer was mainly a defensive weapon, and although many were used in the field in the early part of the war since any weapon that could fire was needed, they saw less and less field use as the war went on.

THE MOUNTAIN HOWITZER

The mountain howitzer was a small, lightweight weapon designed to be broken down and carried by pack animals for use in rugged terrain. While it was not of much use in the east, where it would be subject to counterbattery fire, it was popular in the west especially against Indians who did not have access to artillery. These weapons saw only limited use by Union forces, although the Confederates, especially in the west, employed quite a few of them. They were rarely used in the main actions of the war, however, instead seeing action in places like Carnifix Ferry, West Virginia, in 1861; Glorieta, New Mexico; Giles Court House, West Virginia; and Wood Lake, Minnesota, in 1862. In the latter fight the Federals said that they were used "with great effect" against the Sioux. Regular infantrymen on both sides tended to disregard the weapon. One of the South's leading generals, Patrick Cleburne, reported that during the battle of Richmond, Kentucky, the Union troops: "kept up a ridiculous fire from a little mountain howitzer which they had captured the day before ..."

Most mountain howitzers were used by infantry troops, rather than regular artillery, and acted more as close infantry support weapons than actual artillery. Still, they did appear in the

The M1841 12-pdr. mountain howitzer was designed to be carried in pieces on the backs of three mules. The bronze tube weighed a mere 220 lb., but only had a range of 900 yards at five degrees elevation. It fired a shell weighing almost 9 pounds. They were popular in the west where counterbattery fire was uncommon, but much less so in the east where they were rarely used. The Confederates also cast copies of this weapon. (U.S. Army Ordnance Museum, Aberdeen, Maryland)

A 12-pdr. Dalghren boat howitzer, foreground. The small iron carriage makes the weapon look rather top-heavy. (George Lomas Collection)

ranks. Between August, 1863, and June, 1864, for example, the Atlanta Arsenal issued 14 12-pdr. mountain howitzers, all made by northern foundries and captured from Union forces by the Army of Tennessee.

According to U.S. Army Col. Henry Scott, in his 1861 Military Dictionary, "The mountain howitzer, weight 220 lbs., whole length 37.21 inches, diameter of bore 4.62 inches; length of chamber 2.75 inches, diameter of chamber, 3.34; natural angle of sight, 0.37'; Range 5,000 yards, at an elevation of 2.30', with a charge of 0.5 lb. powder and shell; time of flight, 2 seconds; with the same charge and elevation, the range of spherical-case is 450 yards. At an elevation of from 4.5 to 5.5 the range with canister is 250 yards. According to elevation the range varies from 150 to 1,000 yards; at the same elevation the range with shell being greater than spherical-case. A battery of six mountain howitzers required 33 pack-saddles and harness, and 33 horses or mules. A mountain howitzer ammunition chest will carry about 700 musket ball-cartridges, besides eight rounds for the howitzer."

THE DAHLGREN BOAT HOWITZER

During the Mexican War, the navy took part in a number of landing expeditions, and learned that it needed field artillery of its own. Admiral John Dahlgren, a leading authority on naval artillery, designed a series of boat howitzers that were accepted as the standard U.S. Navy weapon a decade before the Civil War.

These were guns with a bronze tube and a loop under the barrel to secure it either to a field or boat carriage. They were all marked by a lack of a muzzle swell and were available in several sizes, although the 12 lb. shell or shot was common to many of them. The first version had a 4.62-in. bore and weighed 430 lb. by itself and 600 lb. on its special wrought iron carriage.

Detail of the elevating screw and wheel at the end of the carriage of the 12-pdr. Dalghren boat howitzer. (George Lomas Collection)

The medium howitzer had the same bore but weighed 760 lb., or 1,200 lb. on its carriage and was designed for use on frigates. Its range at five degrees was 1,150 yards with case, and 1,085 yards with shell. This was the most popular of this series of cannon.

A lighter version was adopted that weighed 300 lb., while another standard 12-pdr. with a 3.4-in. bore and weighing 880 lb. was also adopted for use on sloops. A light 12-pdr. weighing 300 lb and a rifled bronze 12 pdr. weighing 880 lb were also made during the war. A 20-pdr. with a 4-in. bore and weighing 1,340 lb. was also adopted. During the war a number of rifled 20-pdrs. weighing 1,340 lb. were acquired by the Navy.

The boat howitzer was designed to be mounted on the bow of a launch to fire on an enemy as the boat was making for land. Once the boat hit the shore, a crew of eight to ten men would mount it on its field carriage, an operation that took under four minutes. The weapon was then ready for use in ground-fire support. The carriage came with two ammunition boxes lashed to it, while each crew member also carried two rounds of ammunition in a

The U.S. Navy Dahlgren boat howitzer mounted on its all-metal field carriage. (Bureau of Ordnance, Ordnance Instructions, 1866)

leather pouch. The weapon was landed with a total of 72 rounds of ammunition which was considered more than enough for the typical landing.

The firing rate was eight times a minute – and up to ten times a minute in action – on the carriage, and five times a minute when mounted in the boat. All ammunition was fixed, and the crew had a choice of shell, shrapnel or spherical case, and canister. Powder charges were 1 lb. for the 12-pdr. and 0.625 lb. for the light 12-pounder. The 24-pdr. used a charge of 2 lb., which gave it a range of 1,270 yards for shell and 1,308 yards for shrapnel at five degrees elevation.

The navy acquired 456 medium 12-pdr., 177 light 12-pdr., 23 small 12-pdr., 424 rifled bronze 12-pdr., and seven steel 12-pdr. howitzers (which weighed 790 lb.) during the Civil War in addition to 100 rifled 20-pdrs. and 1,009 24-pdr. boat. howitzers. They had all originally been made by the Washington Navy Yard, but demand forced contracts to go to the private companies Ames and Alger. Due to their unpopularity, the navy ceased acquisition of the small and light boat howitzers early in the war.

Although strictly made for U.S. Navy use, a number of these weapons ended up in army batteries on both sides. At Antietam, for example, they formed part of the ordnance of both Battery K, 9th New York Light Artillery, and Grime's Virginia Battery of the Army of Northern Virginia. They were so popular with the men of Grime's Battery, which was formed in the naval town of Portsmouth, Virginia, that when they were forced to give up one weapon in the overall reorganization, they surrendered a 3-in. Ordnance Rifle rather than the boat howitzer.

WIARD FIELD ARTILLERY

During the war, Norman Wiard, a Canadian by birth, held the job of Superintendent of Ordnance Stores for the U.S. Army. A talented inventor (he also designed and produced special river landing boats for the U.S. government), by 1863 he had developed an entirely new system of field artillery. Wiard's guns used semi-steel, a low carbon cast iron in which some scrap steel was mixed with the pig iron of the charge. The result was a tensile strength of 110,000 lb. per square inch, allowing for smaller barrels that could absorb greater charges. Wiard produced a

A 6-pdr. Wiard rifle. The novel gun with its special carriage is seen from both sides. (Library of Congress)

6-pdr. muzzle-loading rifled gun and a 12-pdr. howitzer that, complete with the unique carriage he also designed, weighed only 1,850 pounds. Beyond that, however, a charge of only 1 oz. of cannon powder would, at an elevation of 35 degrees, throw a 6-lb. shot 800 yards down range. A 2 oz. charge had a range of 1,200 yards, while with a full charge, a shot would travel four miles.

Wiard's carriages were also quite different from the standard carriage design. To withstand the strain of firing at excep-tionally high elevations, the carriage stock was fastened to the underside of the axle. A flat surface plate was placed at the bottom of the trail to limit recoil and indeed, Wiard guns averaged only a 20-in. recoil, about half that of standard cannon. The carriages were smaller and could be nested together, taking only two-thirds the space of a standard field carriage on a ship deck or railroad car.

The carriage wheels were novel in that replaceable parts allowed easy repair. A system of bolts and wedges allowed for repairing the normal shrinkage of a wooden wheel and expansion of a tire, as well as quick repair of combat damage. In one test, Wiard showed that one man could repair the wheels more quickly than another man with an ax could actually damage them. The wheels had "shoes" that could be placed in front or behind a wheel to allow easy descent down steep slopes.

All the Wiard guns were cast at the Trenton, New Jersey, foundry which he owned, the first arriving at a Federal arsenal in December, 1861. The tubes were all marked on the right trunnions "N.W., N.Y.C., O.F."

A detail of the unique carriage used on the Wiard rifle. Carriages could be nestled into each other on railroad flatcars, making it possible to transport more of these weapons on each car than a standard cannon on its carriage. (George Lomas Collection)

It would be satisfying to report that such technologically superior weapons rapidly became the U.S. Army standard. They did not. In all, Wiard sold only 11 batteries, each with four 6-pdr. rifles and two smooth-bore 12-pdr. how-itzers. This was despite the fact that field commanders found the weapons to be highly successful. For example, one Federal commander involved in the action around Charleston, South Carolina, reported in August, 1863 that: "Two Wiard field guns now in position there have proven very destructive to platforms and embrasures; more so than any field guns which have come under my observation." The 12th Ohio Battery brought their Wiard guns into action at

McDowell, Cross Keys, Freeman's Ford, White Sulphur, and the Second Bull Run. At Cross Keys one of the Wiard guns had the wood of the axle torn off, exposing the iron skeleton, but the cannon was fired another 200 times without damage to carriage or axle.

Some of these weapons were captured by Confederates and were issued to their batteries. Two, for example, were sent to the Army of Tennessee in early 1863, but their new owners soon got rid of them in favor of the more common guns.

THE WHITWORTH GUN

The Whitworth breechloading 12-pdr., a British-made gun, was especially designed for long-range use. Tests in England showed that it had a range of 2,600 yards at 5 degrees elevation; at 10 degrees, 4,500 yards; at 20 degrees, 7,000; and at 35 degrees, an astonishing 10,000 yards.

The Whitworth is most associated with the Confederacy, for most of these guns went south. A battery of six 2.75-in. Whitworths, complete with carriages, ammunition, and machinery for making more projectiles was donated to the U.S. government in 1861 by a group of American expatriates. Although these weapons did see limited service on the Peninsula, they were soon installed in the fixed defenses of Washington, never to be fired in anger. Southern forces received the rest of the Whitworths sent to America, and they did use these weapons. The downside, of course, for wide use, was their cost. A single 70-pdr. Whitworth cost £700. This compares to the cost of $515.34, or about £103 at the 1860s exchange rate, for a U.S. Army contract 12-pdr. Napoleon muzzleloader.

The Whitworth also required special ammunition. Two Whitworths shipped to South Australia in 1867 were accompanied by a variety of ordnance: "The projectiles adapted to it consist of solid shot, common and shrapnell [*sic*] shell, rifled spheres and case shot. All the projectiles are made of hard metal and with the exception of the case-shot are rifled by machinery and fit the grooving of the gun." As supplies brought through the blockade did not always reach their destination, the Richmond Arsenal went to work to replicate Whitworth's ammunition. In May, 1863, one of its officials reported that: "The Whitworth shells, fabricated at Richmond, are a decided success; they did admirable execution."

Even with this, the Confederate users found the range and accuracy to be astonishing. Capt. Hardaway opened fire with his battery's 12-pdr. Whitworth on enemy ships at a range of three miles with notable accuracy in December, 1862. At Fredericksburg, as Federals massed for their assault in December, 1862, a Union officer later reported that: "About noon on Sunday they planted a Whitworth gun in the bend of the Massaponax, which annoyed us considerably, throwing its bolts over the whole of the plain. It was so well posted as to be entirely screened from our batteries across the river, and at such a distance, and so hid by trees, as to be hardly discernible by the naked eye. After considerable difficulty, we succeeded in getting the range, which was found to be 2,700 yards with Hall's three guns, and soon silenced it. It did not reopen from that point."

The trick was finding a proper spot for such a long-ranged, accurate weapon. None could be found, for example, in the heavily wooded Chancellorsville campaign until late in the action, when, as a Confederate artillery officer reported:

"The enemy's stragglers were discovered making into the road at a point about 1.5 miles from the river, where the head of a hollow curved around toward Falmouth and kept them out of view until they reached this main ridge. The Whitworth gun of Hardaway's [Hurt's] battery was trained on this point with happy effect. The road was soon cleared of stragglers when an enormous wagon park was discovered about 3 miles distant, where we were told the roads to Aquia Creek and United States Ford branched. Wagons were evidently being concentrated here from United States Ford and Falmouth, while fires of infantry stragglers could be seen occupying every copse around the wagon camp. The range was speedily obtained with Whitworth shell, which operated beautifully, and the utmost consternation seemed to seize upon the teamsters and camp followers. Wagons were seen hurrying off in every direction from the park, while we plied them with solid bolts as long as we thought it would pay. The ammunition being very expensive, we soon desisted."

The Whitworth's main problem for the Confed-

A captured Whitworth rifle, imported by the Confederates from England. These guns were essentially too accurate at too long a range to be wholly effective, given the target acquisition and spotting methods of the period. (Library of Congress)

erates, besides the cost of its ammunition and difficulty of finding a proper place to site it, was the delicacy of its breechloading system in an age when soldiers were not used to mechanical objects. E. P. Alexander, the Chief of Artillery, First Corps, Army of Northern Virginia, recalled that: "The muzzle-loading 6-pdr. and six breech-loading 12-pdr. Whitworths were distributed through the army and often rendered valuable service by their range and accuracy. They fired solid shot almost exclusively, but they were perfectly reliable and their projectiles never failed to fly in the most beautiful trajectory imaginable. Their breech-loading arrangements, however, often worked with difficulty and every one of the six was at some time disabled by breaking of some of its parts, but all were repaired and kept in service. As a general field piece, the efficiency was impaired by its weight and the very cumbrous English carriage on which it was mounted." Indeed, the Whitworth in the Vicksburg garrison burst on the first day of the siege, its cartridge apparently loaded incorrectly.

Confederate ordnance officers also found the Whitworth carriages not only "cumbrous," but also incapable of handling the stress of service. One of the Whitworths in Lee's army broke its axle on the first day, was repaired, and then the same axle broke again under the shock of firing. By 1864 the Richmond Arsenal was producing stronger but lighter carriages for Confederate Whitworths.

Austrian officer FitzGerald Ross summed up the Confederate Whitworth experience in July, 1863: "There are a few Whitworth guns, which are very accurate and of great range, but require much care. The breech has sometimes been blown off or disabled through carelessness in loading. This was especially the case with breech-loading guns. I understand that the Whitworth guns which are now sent out are muzzle-loading. Their field-ammunition the Confederates consider to be far superior to that of the Yankees. Spherical case (shell filled with musket-balls) is the most successful projectile they use."

CONCLUSION

The Civil War began with an emphasis on modernizing artillery; the introduction of the 12-pdr. Napoleon, followed closely by rifled cannon gave cannoneers greater hitting power at greater ranges. But once the war had begun, the emphasis shifted to producing weapons quickly and cheaply for the vast armies in the field. Little or no research or experimentation was carried out on developing breechloading weapons or on the indirect fire control such weapons would need to be effective. The result was that the 12-pdr. Napoleon would continue as the U.S. Army's primary field artillery weapon for many years after the war. It must be admitted, however, that the army's main opponent for decades after the Civil War was the Native American, and their forces were notably lacking in artillery. So the Napoleon was sufficient. In 1918, however, the U.S. found themselves dependent on the French for the bulk of their modern field artillery, with the adoption of the French 75 for the American field artillery.

Where there was development during the war, it was in organization; the armies centralized their artillery which had been

The Confederates imported 32 of these Austrian Army 12-pdr. rifled guns in 1862–63. (Gettysburg National Battlefield Park)

assigned by battery to individual brigades at the start of the war. Both armies organized artillery battalions from individual batteries, and gave their commanders higher ranks than field artillerymen had previously held. This allowed for guns to be massed under one director at important actions. Even this organizational development was not universal. For example, at Gettysburg, the Army of Northern Virginia, which had been able to mass guns well at the Second Manassas, was unable actually to get all of its cannon to fire on the Union line to prepare for Pickett's Charge.

The Confederacy had another problem it was never fully able to overcome, and that was of the quality of southern-made cannon, fuses, and ammunition. The Union ordnance never faced this problem, instead pouring money into northern foundries that continued to build the nation long after the war was over.

GLOSSARY

Canister - a tin cylinder filled with iron balls attached to a sabot and powder bag used in anti-personnel firing.

Cap-square - the iron fittings over a tube's trunnions which secured the tube to the carriage.

Cascabel - the knob on the end of a gun tube.

Case shot - hollow cast-iron shot with musket balls in the center designed as an anti-personnel weapon.

Friction primer - a small tube filled with rifle powder inserted into the vent and fired by pulling a lanyard that drew a rough wire briskly through a friction composition to set off a spark and fire a cannon.

Fuze gouge - a small knife-like device with a wooden handle used to set the cover on the Bormann fuse.

Gunner's level - a brass device much like a spirit level, designed to sit on top of a gun tube with a brass tube holding water with a bubble in it that indicates the angle at which the tube is sitting compared to the center of gravity.

Handspike - a wooden pole that was fitted into the pointing rings at the base of a trail and used to move the piece from side to side as the gunner directed.

Lanyard - a rope with a hook at one end and a wooden handle at the other used to fire a friction primer.

Limber chest - the ammunition chest, its name derived from the fact that it was usually carried on a limber, although it was also carried on a caisson.

Lunette - the iron circle at the rear of a gun's trail that fits into the hook on a limber so it can be pulled.

Pendulum sight (also **pendulum hausse**) - a brass device with an elevating sight that can be moved up and down. The sight is fixed to a holder on the rear of the cannon muzzle, a weight at the bottom keeping it perpendicular to the ground, to sight the cannon. It was carried in a leather pouch worn by the gunner.

Pointing rings - a pair of parallel iron rings on a trail.

Prolonge - a rope usually carried twisted on the trail of the cannon with a hook at one end to fit into the lunette at the rear of a gun's trail, and an iron handle at the other with loops along its length that was used by the cannoneers to pull a gun off a firing line when hooking it to a limber was impossible.

Sabot - a block of wood or metal at the end of a round.

Shell - hollow shot filled with black powder designed to explode and throw fragments into enemy formations.

Solid shot - spherical solid ammunition.

Thumbstall - a piece of padded leather worn on a cannoneer's left thumb to cover the vent during cleaning and loading to prevent air entering the bore and igniting any sparks or powder.

Trunnions - the circular protrusions at the center of balance of a piece that fit onto the carriage to hold a tube on the carriage.

Vent pick - an iron pick, twisted into a circle at one end and sharpened at the other used to pierce the powder bag before the friction primer was inserted to fire the piece.

Worm - an iron corkscrew fitted to the end of a long pole and used to search the bore of a piece after firing to secure all pieces of smoldering powder bags and prevent premature explosions.

SELECT BIBLIOGRAPHY

Alexander, Edward Porter, *Fighting for the Confederacy* (Chapel Hill, North Carolina, 1989)

Andrews, R. Snowden, *Andrews' Mounted Artillery Drill* (Charleston, South Carolina, 1863)

Daniel, Larry J., *Cannoneers in Gray* (University, Alabama, 1984)

Daniel, Larry J., and Riley W. Gunter, *Confederate Canon Foundries* (Union City, Tennessee, 1977)

French, William; Barry, William; Hunt, Henry, *Instruction for Field Artillery* (New York, 1864)

Gorgas, J., *The Ordnance Manual* (Richmond, Virginia, 1862)

Osborn, Thomas, *The Fiery Trail* (Knoxville, Tennessee, 1986)

Poague, William Thomas, *Gunner With Stonewall* (Wilmington, North Carolina, 1987)

Ripley, Warren, *Artillery and Ammunition of the Civil War* (New York, 1970)

Scott, Col. H.L. *Military Dictionary* (New York ,1864)

Tucker, Spencer, *Arming The Fleet* (Annapolis, Maryland, 1989)

Van Loan Naisawald, L., *Grape and Canister* (Washington, D.C., 1960)

Wise, Jennings Cropper, *The Long Arm of Lee, Lincoln*

THE PLATES

A: The caisson and limber attached - a side view.

Each gun had its own limber, plus a spare limber and caisson. The caisson was used to carry two extra limber chests, filled with ammunition. All the extra ammunition, as well as a spare wheel were stored in the limber chests that sat on top of the caisson. Each limber chest was removable, but when filled with ammunition, they were too heavy to be easily moved. Although a gun crew normally walked alongside the gun when it was being moved, they could also ride a caisson and limber. In this case, seated from left as they faced front, the gunner, number six, and number five rode the limber used to pull the gun, while number two, number seven, and number one rode the limber that pulled the caisson. Number four, number eight, and number three rode on the front limber chest of the caisson.

Numbered parts are: 1: stock; 2: side rail; 3: foot board; 4: ammunition chest; 5: spare wheel; 6: axle for spare wheel; 7: chain and toggle; 8: lock chain; 9: spare pole.

B: The 12-pdr. Napoleon gun attached to the limber, a side view.

Generally ammunition enough for a single action could be carried in the limber chest mounted on top of the limber which was also used to haul the gun. Indeed, the limber was essentially the artilleryman's prime mover, as it had the pole for attaching horses, while the hook on the back could be used to haul a gun, a caisson, a battery wagon, or a traveling forge. Rammers and screws used to clean out the gun, were fitted in iron hooks under the gun carriage, while a water bucket, needed to swab out the gun during use hung from the

A limber and caisson stand ready to be hitched up. (Gettysburg National Battlefield Park)

bottom of the carriage and a grease bucket, in which spare grease was carried, hung from the bottom of the limber.

The parts numbered are: 1: handles; 2: ammunition chest; 3: turnbuckle and hasp; 4: corner plates; 5: prolonge; 6: stay pins and keys; 7: pintle hook; 8: axle body; 9: axle tree; 10: pole prop; 11: end bands of splinter bar, trace hooks and pole prop chain; 12: foot boards; 13: pole strap; 14: pole pad; 15: pole yoke; 16: pole.

C: The 12-pdr. Napoleon gun attached to the limber, a top view.

Equipment used with each gun was carried with the gun into action. The prolonge rope, by which the men could pull the gun on the field without having to resort to a horse team, was tied up on top of the carriage trail.

The parts numbered are: 1: prolonge hooks; 2: axle body; 3: nave bands; 4: handspikes and sponges; 5: cap square; 6: head of chin bolts; 7: wheel guard plates; 8: small pointing ring; 9: trail handles; 10: foot boards; 11: pole; 12: splinter bar; 13: lunette; 14: trail plate; 15: large pointing ring.

D: A detailed schematic drawing of the pattern for the 6-pdr. field gun carriage and the tubes it mounted.

The standard U.S. light artillery carriage at the start of the 19th Century used a split or flask trail design, although from as early as 1778 the British had been using a single trail design that offered advantages in terms of ease of construction and a shorter turning radius, with greater mobility.

The French Army adopted the British system in 1827, and the Americans began producing copies of the French

ABOVE **12-pdr. Napoleons near City Point, Virginia, in 1864.
Note the markings on the front of the limber chest.
(Library of Congress)**

BELOW **A battery wagon belonging to the 3rd Battery,
Excelsior Brigade, from New York, at the battery's ordnance
park in Washington. (U.S. Army Military History Institute)**

carriages in 1830, based on drawings obtained by a visiting
U.S. officer in 1829. They were so successful that they were
adopted for the entire service in 1836. The carriage was
officially designated the pattern of 1840.

American carriages came in three sizes, the most popular
one of which was the 6-pounder gun carriage that was used
for Napoleons, Parrott Rifles, 3-in. Ordanance Rifles and
some Blakely and Wiard rifles. The 24-pounder howitzer
carriage was similar but larger, although it was also
sometimes used for Napoleons.

E: A battery wagon. Top and side views with a cutaway of the interior from the top.

Equipment used for the battery was carried in the battery
wagon, along with spare hay for the horses in the forage rack
on its back. Equipment would have included: sabers, which
were issued to all artillerymen but not worn in action by any
but drivers; thumbstalls, used to prevent air from entering the
bore while the weapon was being cleaned and reloaded
between shots; vent picks, used to pierce the fabric powder
bag so that a spark from the friction primer can enter it to
explode the powder; vent cleaning punches, used to clear
out the vent between shots; a pendulum hausse used by the
gunner to aim the cannon by making sure it is level; the
lanyard and friction primers.

Numbered parts (side view) are: 1: lunette; 2: stock;
3: guard plate; 4: lock chain bridle; 5: lock chain; 6: cover
strap and turnbuckle; 7: lock chain hook; 8: bottom rails;
9: side boards; 10: bars of forage rack; 11: forage rack
chains; 12: cover boards.

Numbered parts (top view) are: 1: lunette; 2: stock;
3: spare stock stirrup; 4: hinges; 5: cover boards; 6: bows;
7: cross bars; 8: bottom boards; 9: spare stock hook;

10: sides of forage rack; 11: bars of forage rack; 12: bottom rails.

F: The traveling forge, top and side cutaway views.

Each battery had a traveling forge which was pulled by a limber, and used to reshoe horses and occasionally replace small pieces of iron cannon or limber parts damaged in action. The horseshoes, nails, and anvil were stored in the limber chest, while coal was carried in the chest on the rear of the forge. A vice was attached to the pole that connected the forge to its limber. Within minutes of stopping the forge could be in action, with a farrier assigned to work it.

Numbered parts (side view) are: 1: vice; 2: fireplace; 3: air back; 4: back of fireplace; 5: windpipe; 6: fulcrum and support for bellows pole; 7: bellows; 8: roof of the bellows house; 9: handles; 10: turnbuckle and hasp; 11: coal box; 12: side rail; 13: bellows hook; 14: stock stirrups; 15: stock; 16: prop.

Numbered parts (top view) are: 1: lunette; 2: wheel guard plates; 3: fireplace; 4: air back; 5: bellows hook; 6: fulcrum; 7: hook and staples for carrying bellows pole; 8: roof boards; 9: handles of coal box; 10: hinges of coal box; 11: lid of coal box; 12: bottom boards; 13: bellows; 14: bows; 15: hinges; 16: windpipe; 17: stock.

G: Packed limber boxes.

Both from top and side, showing packed ammunition for, 1: 6-pdr. Gun; 2: 12-pdr. Gun; and 3: 12-pdr. howitzer. In the chests for the 6-pdr. and 12-pdr. gun (the Napoleon) a small tray was fitted so that the ammunition would be snug in the limber chest. It could be used for friction primers, tools, or whatever the section chief or battery commander wanted. The ammunition itself sat on wooden sabots, the ball resting in the sabot. The rounds were attached to cloth, usually flannel, sacks in which the powder was carried. They would be rammed into the tube as a single piece. The larger types of ammunition, one slot of which appears for each gun, were fixed canister rounds, iron balls packed into what was essentially a tin can, that were used for anti-personnel rounds at close ranges.

The battery farrier makes use of the battery forge for some quick horse-shoing in this etching by eyewitness Edwin Forbes.

HEAVY ARTILLERY

INTRODUCTION

Since heavy artillery made up the first line of defense of the United States, more attention was paid to it, and money spent on it, than on field artillery. In 1855, for example, the Chief of Ordnance reported having acquired 54 10-inch columbiads and 68 8-inch columbiads. During the same year, for comparison, the army only acquired 39 bronze field guns and two bronze howitzers of all calibers. In all, the army installed 224 heavy seacoast and garrison guns, mostly in the San Francisco area, although a number went to a new fort at Key West. In 1855, the U.S. Army's ordnance park of 10-inch and 8-inch howitzers and seacoast howitzers numbered 2,319, with another 2,957 seacoast and garrison guns. There were also 269 mortars.

In January, 1860, there were 61 forts and batteries that defended America's coastal cities. However, very few of these were actually garrisoned, even though the forts were armed and, in theory, ready for action. Of all the forts along the southern coast that would face takeover in 1861, only three were manned: Fort Taylor, Key West, Florida, had a garrison of 52 men; Fort Sumter, South Carolina, had a garrison of 89 men; and Fort Pickens, Pensacola, Florida, had a garrison of 59 men. The others had either only an ordnance sergeant or fort-keeper on hand to maintain the fort and its guns or were totally abandoned.

Many of the guns of the United States fell into Confederate hands when the undermanned forts along the southern seacoast were taken over by local authorities. As the U.S. Secretary of War reported to Congress in June, 1861, "The Government arsenals at Little Rock, Baton Rouge, Mount Vernon, Apalachicola, Augusta, Charleston, and Fayetteville, the ordnance depot at San Antonio and all the other Government works in Texas, which have served as the depots of immense stores of arms and ammunition, have been surrendered by the commanders or seized by

A 32-pounder columbiad gun in a casemate of Fort Delaware, typical of all prewar coastal defense forts build along the Atlantic coast of the United States.

disloyal hands. Forts Macon, Caswell, Johnston, Clinch, Pulaski, Jackson, Marion, Barraneas, McRee, Morgan, Gaines, Pike, Macomb, Saint Philip, Livingston, Smith, and three at Charleston; Oglethrope Barracks, Barraneas Barracks, New Orleans Barracks, Fort Jackson on the Mississippi; the battery at Bienvenue, Dupré, and the works at Ship Island, have been successively stolen from the Government or betrayed by their commanding officers." With the sea forts, especially, came large stores of heavy artillery pieces. The Confederacy would start off on fairly equal terms with the Union in the area of heavy artillery, a rare exception to all other areas in which the North largely predominated.

The rear of Fort Delaware's 32-pounder columbiad shows how the carriage can be pivoted to be aimed.

On April 20, 1861, the new Confederate Ordnance Department surveyed what they had acquired in their capture of federal forts. According to Major Josiah Gorgas, Chief of Ordnance, their park included: "Ten-inch columbiads, 8; 8-inch columbiads, 41; 24-pounder guns, 191; 24-pounder guns (flank defense), 9; 32-pounder guns, 188; 24-pounder howitzers (flank defense), 37; 10-inch mortars, 19; 6-pounder field guns, 2; 42-pounder guns, 48; 18-pounder guns, 5; 12-pounder guns, 2; 8-inch sea-coast howitzers, 13; 8-inch navy guns, 2; 13-inch mortars, 2; Coehorn mortars, 6, and 9-inch navy guns, 2; in fortifications, 375.

"At arsenals – Thirty-two pounder guns, 40; 24-pounder guns, 3; 24-pounder howitzers (for flank defense), 6, and 8- and 10-inch mortars, 5; total in fortifications and arsenals, 429."

These were not always the newest of guns. For example, Fort Macon, North Carolina, received its first iron 24-pounders in 1835–36, and these tubes were to be put to use in 1861. Over the years, the wooden gun carriages had rotted away, having received only minimal refurbishing. When the Confederates took over, they found four guns mounted on carriages rebuilt in 1844, while another 13 guns lay on skids on the fort's wharf. There would be much to do to get this, and the other Southern coastal forts into shape for defense.

On November 15, 1863, Gorgas, by then a colonel, reported that Southern sources had begun producing heavy artillery, the chief source being the Tredegar Iron Works in Richmond. By then, the Confederate army had received 31 heavy guns from Southern sources, and bought another 46 heavy guns from outside suppliers both in the South and abroad.

The army of Northern Virginia corps artillery chief, E. Porter Alexander, described a typical Confederate heavy artillery defense as a mixture of prewar columbiads and Southern-made big guns: "The heavy

A columbiad in a casemate under fire at Fort Sumter.

guns which defended the James River against the enemy's fleet were principally the ordinary eight-inch and ten-inch columbiads, and 'Brooke's rifles' of six and four tenths and seven inches caliber. These rifles only needed telescopic sights (which could not be made in the Confederacy) to be perfect arms of their class, their trajectories being more uniform than the sighting of the guns could be made by the eye. In addition to these rifles Captain Brooke also furnished some heavily banded smoothbores of ten and eleven inches caliber, to fire wrought-iron balls with very high charges against the ironclads, which would doubtless have been extremely effective at short ranges."

Even after losing all the guns it did to the seceding Southerners, the U.S. Army had a lot of heavy artillery remaining at its disposal and a much greater manufacturing capacity that could easily replace what it had lost and more. At the outbreak of hostilities, the U.S. Ordnance Department counted 544 siege guns on hand, and, by June 30, 1862, had added 211 siege guns, for a total of 755. Similarly, it had 1,508 seacoast guns at the beginning of the war, and by June 30, 1862, had acquired 302 more guns for a total of 1,810. A year later the U.S. Army had on hand 1,090 siege guns and 1,926 seacoast guns and mortars. During the year between June 30, 1863, and June 30, 1864, the Ordnance Department reported issuing another 604 siege guns and 1,127 seacoast guns and mortars. Finally, on June 30, 1864, the Ordnance Department reported that a year earlier it had on hand 346 siege guns and mortars, had acquired another 424, issued 32, and had on hand 738 of these weapons. As to seacoast guns and mortars, it had 812 on hand a year earlier, acquired 612, issued 593, and had 831 seacoast guns and mortars left over.

Union forces had a different heavy artillery problem than did the Confederates, who merely had to use their heavy artillery for defense. First, Union forces needed their heavy guns in defensive fortifications, not only inland as around Washington, D.C., but along the coast as at Fort Warren, Boston; Fort Jay, New York; and Fort Delaware, Delaware City. Second, Union forces needed heavy artillery to besiege Confederate forts.

COLUMBIADS

The columbiad is a type of gun dating from the beginning of the 19th century and is considered the first piece of purely American-designed ordnance. It first saw service in the War of 1812, both on ships and with the army, and came in 24-pounder, 50-pounder, and 100-pounder sizes. In 1811, the first 50-pounder columbiads appeared for use as seacoast guns, followed by the 100-pounder columbiads in 1819. Originally, these were short, large-bore cannon used to fire solid shot and were made with a chamber at the base of the bore like a howitzer. In 1844, the weapon was redesigned to accept a larger powder charge by lengthening the tube and increasing the tube's weight. In practice, this did not work, and the previous size charges remained the standard. A further change was made in 1858 with the removal of the muzzle swell and base ring. The powder chambers were also eliminated.

Columbiads were made with elevating ratchets that ran all the way up the face of the breech, permitting elevation to 39°, rather than the 15° elevation possible for a gun that used an elevating screw or quoins placed under the breech.

Columbiads had become larger by the Civil War. According to Colonel Henry Scott, writing in 1861, the columbiad was: "An American cannon invented by Colonel [George] Bomford [1780 - 1848], of very large caliber, used for throwing solid shot or shells, which, when mounted in barbette, has a vertical field of fire from 5° depression to 39° elevation, and a horizontal field of fire of 360°. Those of the old pattern were chambered, but they are now cast without, and otherwise greatly improved. The 10-inch [128-pounder] weighs 15,400 lbs., and is 126 inches long. The 8-inch columbiad [64-pounder] is 124 inches long and weighs 9,240 lbs. Rodman's 15-inch columbiad [49, 100 lbs] ... was cast at Pittsburgh, Pennsylvania, by Knapp, Rudd & Co., under the directions of Captain T.J. Rodman, of the Ordnance Corps, who conceived the design, which he has happily executed, of casting guns of large size hollow, and by means of a current of water introduced into the core, which forms the mold of the bore, cooling it from the interior, and thus making the metal about the bore of the hardest and densest, and giving the whole thickness of metal subjected to internal strain its maximum strength."

The Rodman method of casting was developed in the mid-1840s and consisted of cooling the gun from the inside out to improve stress resistance when firing. An army officer, Rodman offered the casting system to the Ordnance Department, but was turned down. He then went into business with Charles Knapp of the Fort Pitt Foundry, which began casting guns made by this system. As it turned out, Rodman's calculations were correct, and as a result larger columbiads could be cast, using the Rodman system, than could have been before. Rodman-cast guns have smooth, flowing lines, and as a result many period cannoneers incorrectly called the 3-inch Ordnance Rifles "Rodman guns."

The major Southern cannon founders, the Tredegar Iron Works and the Bellona Foundry, both in Virginia, had, before the war, rejected the Rodman casting system. As a result, they were limited in the size of columbiads they could cast. Tredegar finally learned to use the Rodman casting method, and in November, 1864, finally

This smoothbore in Port Royal, South Carolina, is mounted on the standard wooden carriage. Notice how it is elevated by means of quoins, or wedges with handles, shoved between the bottom of the tube and the top of the carriage. The carriage is mounted on a center pintle so that it can be revolved in a complete circle. (Library of Congress)

Prewar smoothbores pressed into service by the Confederates and mounted in the water battery along the Mississippi River at Vicksburg. The vents are covered to protect them from the weather by metal caps secured to the tube with leather straps. (Library of Congress)

cast a 12-inch gun using this system. However, it was too late in the war to produce such guns in any numbers. The 15-inch columbiad requested in 1861 from Tredegar was never produced. One of Tredegar's first efforts, a 6.4-inch columbiad, was sent to the defenses of Savannah, where it blew up on the first shot, killing two and wounding several others. Robert E. Lee, an observer, was narrowly missed by one of the pieces of the gun.

Bellona, although it never did cast any guns with the Rodman system, produced some 15 8-inch and 10-inch columbiads in 1862, until its production was interrupted by a fire in the foundry. By June, 1863, production of columbiads at Bellona resumed, but in 1863 the foundry delivered only 12 10-inch columbiads, along with two 7-inch guns and two 9-inch guns. A 10-inch Bellona columbiad in the West Point collection bears the serial number 67 and an 1864 date.

In September, 1861, a Natchez, Tennessee, newspaper reported: "An 8-inch columbiad has been manufactured at the foundry of Messrs. Bennett & Lurges of New Orleans under the superintendence of Mr. Daniel Brasill, according to the most approved pattern. It was cast solid and bored. The time occupied in boring was two weeks, and when it was tested, according to the general rules for that purpose, it was found to stand 'all that could be put upon it.' Shells were thrown from it without straining, a distance of a full two miles." Before New Orleans fell, the company cast five of these guns, each weighing 11,000 pounds.

Noble Brothers & Co., Rome, Georgia, cast several columbiads, but these were rejected by the Confederate Ordnance Department for faulty casting.

In terms of range, Colonel Scott reported of the gun at Fort Monroe: "The mean ranges at 6° elevation, of ten shots, was 1,936 yards, and the mean lateral deviation 2.2 yards; 35 lbs. of .6-inch grain powder being the charge and 7" the time of flight. At 10° elevation and 40 lbs. of powder, large grain, the range was 2,700 yards, and the time of flights 11".48. At 28° 35' elevation the range was 5,730 yards; time of flight 27", and the lateral deviation, as observed with a telescope attached to one of the trunnions, very slight."

On the Confederate side, Major Edward Manigault, commander of the Siege Train, Charleston garrison, reported on typical firing patterns with an 8-inch columbiad on August, 17, 1863, "… opened fire at 11 A.M. from the 8 in columbiad in Battery Haskell. According to instructions directed the fire entirely on the heavy Rifle Batteries to South of the House on Morris Island known as Graham's Hd. Quarters.

Fired 27 shots from this columbiad in course of day. With 8 lb. cartridges, average elevation of 22° 30". With 10 lb. cartridges, an average elev. of 20°. The practice was not good and all the shells failed to burst except about three."

The Confederates also tried turning prewar smoothbore columbiads into more modern rifled pieces, apparently with some success. On January 9, 1864, General P.G.T. Beauregard wrote Colonel Josiah Gorgas, Chief of Ordnance, the results of experiments in ordnance tried at Charleston, in which he commanded: "I have delayed answering your letter of the 27th November, 1863, referring to the rifling and banding of 8-inch and 10-inch columbiads, until I could carefully reconsider my preconceived views and subject them to the test of actual experiment.

"Up to this time, however, the enemy have not given me an opportunity of trying the 10-inch rifled and banded columbiads as fully as I desire; but so far the results with the 8-inch rifled and banded pieces have been most satisfactory. Your letter alludes chiefly to the 10-inch gun, but as your objections and conclusions must apply equally to the 8-inch as to the 10-inch, I must acquaint you that an 8-inch gun, rifled and double banded, in position at Fort Moultrie, has been fired through some four or five different engagements, in all over 100 times, with shell weighing over 100 pounds and bolts 140 pounds, with most satisfactory results, giving a greater range with the same charges and less elevation than the smoothbore, with shell and shot of less than half the weight. The gun is uninjured, and there is no apparent reason why it should not last a long time.

"It is regarded by Gen. Ripley as the best gun in the battery, and in action has an immediate effect upon the enemy's ironclads, which always try to avoid it.

"This having proved a success, three others of the same kind have been prepared and placed in position in the harbor batteries, but owing to the limited supply of projectiles a thorough test has not been applied. The charges used have been 8 pounds and 10 pounds of coarse-grained powder, and the range shows these to have been sufficient to give full velocity to the projectiles for distances of 1,000 yards.

A Confederate naval gun at Yorktown. Note the solid shot piled up behind it within easy reach of the crew.

"The experiment on 10-inch columbiads was first made with one which had a trunnion knocked off at Fort Sumter, and the rifling and banding of which was executed by a private firm. Another one was banded at the arsenal and rifled by the same parties who altered the first one. When finished I had the former mounted on Sullivan's Island and the latter on James Island. Gen. Ripley writes as follows touching both:

"They have both been tried, the latter (One at

A 32-pounder seacoast gun at Fort Slemmer, Arlington Heights, Virginia, part of the defenses of Washington. The man in front of the carriage wears a gunner's pouch in which he carries friction primers to fire the gun, and holds a lanyard tight, apparently ready to fire. (Library of Congress)

Fort Johnson, banded at the arsenal) with a projectile invented by Capt. Harding, weight[ing] about 215 pounds, and a Parrott projectile, weight[ing] about 250 pounds, and charges of 15 pounds and 16 pounds. With the latter, excellent results were obtained. The former projectiles failed generally to take the grooves, and with 16 pounds broke up. The practice I have been informed has been delayed by the starting of one of the bands which was defectively welded, the gun itself being uninjured.

"The other gun has been fired with 12 and 15 pounds of powder with Harding's projectiles only, others not having been furnished. Twelve hundred yards was obtained with $2\frac{1}{2}$ degrees elevation and 12 pounds large-grained powder, when the projectiles took the grooves. With 15 pounds the projectile broke. The gun thus far is uninjured, and I have no doubt will continue so under any ordinary practice. This will be continued as soon as Parrott projectiles can be procured.

"If Parrott shot are provided, range, accuracy, weight, and velocity are obtained with safe charges, and from the effect of the 8-inch bolts on the monitors I believe one or two well-directed shots from the 10-inch rifles will drive any one of them out of action, and half a dozen permanently damage and sink them.

"The two 10-inch columbiads selected for experiment weighed over 15,000 pounds before they were double-banded, and afterward, respectively, 22,000 pounds and 20,000 pounds.

"The guns selected for the purpose were captured at Forts Moultrie and Sumter in April, 1861, of the very best iron, and superior to those now manufactured by the Ordnance Department of the Confederate States. I do not say that these rifled and banded 8 and 10 inch guns are the best that can be made of their calibers, but, in my belief, they are the best we can get in the present condition of our manufacturing resources. It is proper to add that the number of guns at our disposal of the proper description for alteration is limited."

Columbiads were initially placed on standard wooden carriages. However, an all-iron carriage was developed by the Union army and this was described by Colonel Scott: "The gun is mounted upon the new iron center pintle carriage, which with requisite lightness has great strength and stiffness; and to facilitate the pointing from 5° depression to 39° elevation, a slot is cut in the knob of the cascabel, and a ratchet is formed on the base of the breech to receive a 'pawl' attached to the elevating screw. If the distance be greater than the length of a single notch of the ratchet, the piece is rapidly moved by a lever which passes through an opening in the pawl. If the distance is less, than the elevating screw is used. The piece was fired and maneuvered during the trials at Fort Monroe, with great facility, being manned by 1 sergeant and 6 negroes; the times of loading were 1'15" and 1'3". Time in traversing 90° 2'20", and in turning back 45° 1". Time of loading, including depressing and elevation, 4' and 3'18"." The Confederate Army lacked the facilities and even raw materials for such carriages and depended on the older wooden carriages for their siege guns.

At the siege of Fort Pulaski, three 10-inch columbiads recoiled off their pintles (the iron pins that fastened the carriage front to the platform, allowing the rear to roll on a traverse track) on their first shots. It turned out that the guns were mounted on the new iron carriages, but the pintles were the old wooden carriage type that did not work with the new carriages.

Nor could the iron carriages easily be used for besieging Confederate positions where Union troops had to drag the giant guns into position. Lieutenant-Colonel Joseph R. Hawley, 7th Connecticut, wrote of the

This 32-pounder at Fort Richardson, Virginia, is mounted on a carriage. As such, it could be moved with field forces, the heaviest gun in the American arsenal that could be moved easily. It would see use at places such as Fredericksburg in December, 1862. (Library of Congress)

The near 32-pounder has been mounted on a naval carriage, while the one in the distance sits on a wooden garrison carriage.

siege of Georgia's Fort Pulaski: "[as] A columbiad weighs from 13,000 to 15,000 pounds, it has been no light job to drag them up there, the wheels sometimes sinking to the axle and the tugging procession sneaking along an open beach within 1,600 to 2,000 yards of the scores of guns in Pulaski and nothing but a placid bay between."

As with all guns, especially when it was impossible to x-ray tubes to determine defects, there was danger in firing even usually reliable columbiads. When giant guns like columbiads burst, everyone around was endangered. Confederate Major Edward Manigault reported such an event from the defenses of Charleston on September 18, 1863: "At the 12th Shot and at 5 H. 10 M. P.M. the 8 inch [seacoast] Columbiad burst … The columbiad was fired with 10 lbs of powder, a solid Shot, and at an elevation of $19\frac{1}{2}$ degrees when it burst. The Cartridge & Shot were reported as being 'home'." At the previous discharge, the Shell had burst about 10 or 30 feet in front of the Gun. From a point 2 ft. in front of the center of the Trunnions, the Chase remains perfect. The Body & breech of the gun is separated into two equal portions, the plane of Fracture being vertical and directly through the vent & axis of the Bore. One of these pieces was thrown over a house 10 ft. high and fell to the Right at a distance of 75 ft. from the Chassis. The other half was thrown to the left crushing the leg of Private [Wade] Mills [Co. K, 2d S.C. Artillery] against the Stump of a Cedar Tree and fell at a distance of 30 ft. from the Chassis. The Gun Carriage was destroyed; the Chassis uninjured.

"This gun has been fired by us about 393 Times, with an average elevation of 20°. The Charge usually 10 lbs of Powder and a Columbiad Shell [50 lbs.]. But occasionally 8 lb. charges were used with an Encreased Elevation of about 2 degrees. Also some 8 in. Solid Shot have been fired. The Bore appeared to be as perfect as possible, with the exception of a very slight hollow or 'lodgement' a little in front (5 in.) of the Chamber ($\frac{1}{32}$ in. deep, say) and a slight 'score' in the Chase part of the Bore. The vent was somewhat enlarged and irregular but to no great extent.

"I have been informed by a well instructed Ordnance Officer of great experience (Captain, now Genl. Boggs) that the Guns of 1855 & 1856 had generally proved not to be guns of much endurance.

"The Marks upon the Gun were as follows:

"Right Trunnion marked R.P.P. [stamped above] W.P.F. Left Trunnion, 1855. On the Breech, 9206. On Muzzle, No. 80 [at top] B.H. [at left]. Near the Trunnion, sight Mass, U.S."

HOWITZERS

Howitzers used for siege and garrison work were cast iron and came in two sizes, 24-pounder and 8-inch. The 24-pounder was already an old weapon by the beginning of the war, having been introduced in 1839, although apparently not produced until several years later. The main job for the 24-pounder howitzer was as a weapon placed on the flanks of fortifications to protect against infantry attack, rather than for use in counter-battery operations. As such, it was usually mounted on a flank casemate carriage.

The 8-inch siege howitzer was introduced in 1841 and came with a cylindrical chamber that joined the bore with a spherical curve that fit a shell exactly. The powder chamber held exactly four pounds of powder, the standard charge. The weapon was designed to be used mainly to smash into masonry and earth left over after fortification walls had been penetrated by larger guns. The 8-inch howitzer was also designed for ricochet firing.

The 8-inch howitzer could be mounted on a 24-pounder carriage. However, when that was done, the elevating screw had to be removed and the cannoneers use a quoin for adjusting the elevation. The howitzer barrel was just too short to rest on the screw, being only 46.5 inches long. Even with quoins, it could be elevated at a very high elevation, giving the weapon a maximum range of some 1,600 yards and a minimum range of 300 yards.

The army also had an 8-inch seacoast howitzer that was introduced in 1839. It had a 93-inch-long tube. Officially it had been dropped from the rolls by 1861, but in fact many of these weapons were in the fortifications of both sides. As well, a 10-inch seacoast howitzer was adopted at the same time as the 8-inch version, but with a 101.5-inch tube, and was dropped from rolls at the same time as the smaller piece.

Howitzers also saw improvised use. In 1866, the Army of Northern Virginia corps artillery chief, E. Porter Alexander, recalled that: "On several occasions during 1863, and 1864, where mortar fire was desirable in the field, the twelve and twenty-four pounder howitzers were used for the purpose very successfully, by sinking the trails in trenches to give the elevation, while the axles were run up on inclined skids a few inches to lift the wheels from the ground and lessen the strain of the recoil. The skids would not be necessary where the desired range is not great."

This 32-pounder naval gun has been adapted by the Confederates to hold a heavier charge than usual by placing a band around the breech. It was part of the defenses of Vicksburg. (Library of Congress)

RIFLED GUNS

The U.S. Army's M1861 4.5-inch siege rifle and the M1862 4.62-inch siege rifle were 12-pounder weapons that saw wide use on both sides. The U.S. Army also developed its M1861 4.5-inch siege rifle, a weapon that looked much like a 3-inch Ordnance Rifle but was made of cast, not wrought, iron. One Union artillery expert later reported that: "The two siege batteries of 4.5-inch ordnance guns which accompanied the Army of the Potomac in all its movements from Fredericksburg were of great use from their superior range and accuracy, in silencing troublesome field batteries and in other field service and could be moved with the reserve artillery without impeding the march of the army …" The weapon, using a 3.25-pound charge behind a 25.5-pound patent Dyer shell at 10° elevation, had a range of some 3,265 yards. The 30-pound Hotchkiss or Schenkl projectiles were the most commonly used ammunition for this piece.

Confederate officials also produced similar iron siege rifles, with the Tredegar Iron Works in Richmond casting its first 8-inch rifle in June, 1861, its first 9-inch rifle that July, its first 10-inch rifle and its first 32-pounder rifle that November, and its first 4.62-inch rifle in December, 1862.

On August 30, 1863 Confederate Major Edward Manigault, on the defenses of Charleston, noted: "Late this afternoon Received at Battery Haskett one 4.62 in. Rifle Siege Gun. Weight 5,750 lbs. Marked B.F. [Bellona Foundry] J.L.A. [Junius L. Archer, foundry owner] 1862. Band [reinforcing band over the breech] 19 in. long x 2 in. thick. Gun & Carriage look new. Siege Carriage." This was but one of several such guns Manigault's defenses owned, and they were his favorite guns. For example, he wrote on September 4, 1863, that: "The 4.62 Rifle is by far the most accurate and reliable one we have …" Bellona does not appear to have produced Brooke rifles, so this weapon is likely to be a copy of the earlier U.S. Army 4.62-inch siege rifle.

As far as capabilities, he noted on August 20, 1863: "Fired 20 Shots from 4.62 in. Rifle Siege Gun twelve of which were directed to Morris Island and eight at the Mud Battery in the Marsh S.E. from Legare's Point. With 3 pnd. Charge of powder the 4.62 in. Rifle required about 20° Elevation to reach Morris Island and 10 $\frac{1}{2}$ deg. to reach Mud Fort in Marsh."

As with any large guns, mishaps could happen with the 4.62-inch siege rifle. On August 22, 1863, Manigault recorded: "At 2:20 P.M. the 4.62 in Rifle Siege Gun on Platform No. 1 burst. The breech was blown out without any other damage being done. The Bands were neither broken nor

One of the 32-pounders at Fort Fisher after the fort's bombardment and eventual capture. Note how the carriage has been set up so that it can be moved easily from side to side. (Library of Congress)

thrown off and the rear one only somewhat loosened." Generally, however, the guns were durable. He recorded that on August 30, 1863: "Up to 3 P.M. today the 4.62 Rifle has been fired 155 times and the vent is much enlarged and somewhat ragged on the outside."

Charles T. James, a U.S. senator before the war, designed a system of rifling bronze smoothbore guns, as well as a totally unique 14-pounder bronze (a few of steel) rifle for the U.S. Army. These largely date from 1861 - 62, the year in which James was killed in an accident involving one of his experimental guns. James rifles in 24-, 32-, and 42-pounder sizes were used by Union forces, including those that took Fort Pulaski, where they were considered highly effective. In appearance they were smoothly tapered tubes that resembled 3-inch Ordnance Rifles.

A row of columbiads at the Confederate water battery of Fort Johnson in Charleston Harbor. Damage to the near carriage seems to have been deliberate. (Library of Congress)

PARROTT RIFLES

A West Point graduate, Robert P. Parrott, who had resigned his commission in 1836 to head a private foundry, designed a tube that could be used for both siege guns and field artillery. Essentially, his cast-iron tube had a wrought-iron reinforcing wedge-shaped band wrapped around the breech with the joints pounded together until welded shut. In the process, the tube was rotated on rollers, a stream of water being shot inside to keep the tube cool as the hot band was wrapped around it. Because the tube rotated, the band cooled and clamped itself uniformly to the breech, instead of being tighter where the weight pulled the band down on the top of a stationary piece, while the bottom part was less tightly bound to the tube.

This band allowed the breech to absorb greater stress than an unbanded, or even typically banded, cannon. Indeed, the weapon was known as a tough cannon that could take a beating and remain in use. It was easy and cheap to produce, which was important in a war as large as was the Civil War. They were produced at the West Point Foundry under Parrott's supervision.

The Parrott's main problem was the tendency for the tube to explode in use, usually just in front of the band, after prolonged service. In October, 1865, the Chief of Ordnance reported that: "The many failures, by bursting, of the celebrated Parrott guns in the land and naval service have weakened confidence in them, and make it the imperative duty of this department to seek elsewhere for a more reliable rifle gun." The larger the Parrott, the more liable it was to burst.

A columbiad at Confederate Fort McAllister, outside Savannah, Georgia. Note the ammunition, solid shot, piled up for ready use. The weapon can be rotated through 360° on its platform and track. (Library of Congress)

Confederate Major Edward Manigault, in the defenses of Charleston, wrote on August 19, 1863: "At the 13th Round the 30 pndr. Parrott Gun burst. One man badly stunned, and one slightly so. No other damage done." On the Union side, in the same siege, a 30-pounder cast in 1863 fired 4,606 rounds, an average of 127 rounds a day, at a range of 6,600 yards when it finally burst into seven pieces. The real problem was that it was impossible to tell exactly when a Parrott would burst. For example, of two apparently identical 100-pounder Parrotts firing into Charleston, one burst on the 122d round, while the other lasted until the 1,151st round.

Heavy Parrotts also had a tendency to break their elevating screws, due to the weight being distributed on the rear of the tube. With all this, the chief engineer in the Union Army outside Charleston reported that: "There is perhaps no better system of rifled cannon than Parrot's [*sic*]; certainly none more simple in construction, more easily understood or that can, with more safety, be placed in the hands of inexperienced men for use."

The first Parrott, a 10-pounder, was produced in 1860 and the weapons went into full production in 1861. For siege purposes, the West Point works produced a number of 30-, 100- (6.4-inch), 200- (8-inch), three 300- (10-inch), and even a 600-pounder version of the light-weight field weapon. The U.S.-issue weapons are marked with a date and the initials RPP and WPF. The 4.2-inch, or 30-pounders, the smallest heavy Parrotts, came in two versions. The first version had a doorknob-shaped cascabel and a muzzle swell; these were produced through 1862. Later versions had a more elongated cascabel and a straight muzzle.

In 1862 alone, the U.S. Army bought 344 Parrott guns of various sizes. Indeed, by that year's end, the Army bought 411 Parrott field guns, 108 siege guns, and 38 seacoast defense guns. The Parrott was thus among the most common of all Union field pieces, despite its problems.

The ease of making such cannon did not escape the Confederates, and J.R. Anderson & Co. cast copies of them at its Tredegar Iron Works in Richmond beginning in November, 1861. The first ones they cast were 6-pounder versions of the weapon, a bore size they continued producing through August, 1862. In July they cast their first 30-pounder Parrott copy. Starting in August, 1863, the Macon Arsenal cast some 20- and 30-pounder Parrotts as well. The Selma Naval Gun Foundry, Alabama, cast at least a dozen 30-pounder Parrott rifles for use on ships and harbor and river defenses.

The larger Tredegar Parrotts saw action at Fredericksburg, where the two 30-pounders sent to Lee's army burst after prolonged firing, one after 39 rounds and the other after 54 rounds. "This was the only time in the war that we ever had such heavy guns in the field," recalled E. Porter Alexander, First Corps artillery chief in the Army of Northern Virginia. "At one of the explosions Genls. Lee & Longstreet & many staff officers were standing very near, & fragments flew all about them, but none was hurt."

A 16-inch Rodman gun in the defenses of Washington, DC.

MORTARS

The mortar is a snub-nosed, smoothbore weapon designed to hurl a ball a great distance into the air so it falls almost vertically into an enemy position. Usually mounted on heavy wooden beds most fell into the definition of siege or heavy artillery, although some were relatively small. The rounds fired were largely designed for use against personnel rather than objects such as masonry walls or enemy artillery. Hence, the preferred ammunition included shells (the primary round), grape, light and fire balls, and carcasses.

According to Colonel Henry Scott's 1861 *Military Dictionary*: "The following mortars are used in the United States service: The heavy 13-inch mortar, weighing 11,500 lbs., the whole length 53 inches, length of chamber 13 inches, and superior diameter of chamber 9.5 inches; the heavy 10-inch mortar, weighing 5,775 lbs., whole length 46 inches, length of chamber 10 inches; the light 10-inch mortar, weighing 1,852 lbs., the whole length of mortar 28 inches, length of chamber 5 inches; the light 8-inch mortar, weighing 930 lbs., whole length of mortar 22.5 inches, length of chamber 4 inches; brass stone mortar, weighing 1,500 lbs., diameter of bore 16 inches, whole length of mortar 31.55 inches, length of chamber 6.75 inches; brass Coehorn 24-pounder, diameter of the bore 5,82 inches, weight 164 lbs., whole length

A 16-inch Rodman gun at Fort McHenry National Park, Baltimore. These guns served as weapons defending the city through World War I.

16.32 inches, length of chamber 4.25 inches; iron eprouvette, diameter of the bore 5,655 inches, weight 220 lbs., length of bore exclusive of diameter, 11.5 inches, length of chamber, 1.35 inch. Mortars are mounted on beds, and when used, siege mortars are placed on a platform of wood made of 6 sleepers, 18 deck planks; and 72 dowels; fastened with 12 iron eye-bolts."

The M1861 10-inch mortar used a charge of one pound six ounces of powder to fire a 104-pound round (27 12-pounder iron canister balls and a bursting charge of 2.5 pounds of powder), 800 yards with a 13-second flight.

Lieutenant-Colonel Joseph R. Hawley, 7th Connecticut, watched the mortars in use at the siege of Fort Pulaski, Georgia. According to him: "… the twelve big mortars will each fire five times an hour (it is a slow job to clean, load and aim them) making 60 shells an hour. Each mortar gives two reports, the firing of the mortar and the bursting of the shell."

In order to give the mortar some mobility during the siege of Petersburg, Union forces used a novel system. According to one of their artillerymen: "The great weight of the 13-inch mortar (17,000 pounds) renders it difficult to move and some satisfactory experiments were made with a novel platform. An ordinary railroad platform car (eight wheels) was strengthened by additional beams tied strongly by iron rods and was plated on top with iron. The mortar was placed upon the car (top of mortar nine feet above the tracks) and run down on the Petersburg and City Point Railroad to a point near our lines where a curve in the track afforded facilities for changing the plane of fire by advancing the car or drawing it back.

"The mortar fired with 14 pounds of powder recoiled less than two feet on the car which moved 10 or 12 feet on the track. The effect of the charge was taken up without damage to the axles, even when a full allowance of 20 pounds of powder was used …

"Its practice was excellent … of course with this platform, the plane of fire must be nearly paralleled to the track or the mortar will be dismounted, but by placing the car on a curve, a very considerable traverse can be secured without difficulty."

The light mortar most used during the war was the M1841 bronze Coehorn mortar, which weighed about 296 pounds on its bed (164 pounds for the tube alone), fired a 24-pounder shell, with a half-pound powder charge, some 1,200 yards. It was manned by a crew of four.

Tredegar cast its first mortar, a 10-inch model, in July, 1862, the first of 10 made that year. Another eight were cast in 1863, five in 1864, and one in 1865 for a total of 24 10-inch mortars. It cast its first 8-inch mortar in February, 1863, and thereafter cast a total of 15, most in late 1864. The Richmond-based foundry was the only major source of Southern-made siege mortars, although a private company, S. Wolff & Co., produced two 10-inch mortars in New Orleans. These were tossed into a canal basin on the fall of that city. A.N. Miller, a foundry in Savannah, produced one 15-inch and three 10-inch seacoast mortars in 1862 for that city's defenses. The Selma Naval Gun Foundry, Alabama, produced 19 Coehorn mortars.

Confederate makers also produced a 12-pounder iron Coehorn mortar which they felt was an effective weapon. According to one Union artillery officer who examined a captured version of this weapon: "For practice against troops, the 12-pounder Coehorn is decidedly more deadly than the 24-pounder as its shell, when the fuse burns too slowly, does not bury itself on striking and the fragments thus scatter widely."

In 1866, the Army of Northern Virginia corps artillery chief, E. Porter Alexander, described the variety of mortars Southern field armies used: "During the siege of Petersburg a number of iron twelve and twenty-four pounder Coehorn mortars were made and rendered excellent service. Wooden mortars were also made and tried for short ranges, but even when they did not split, the ranges were so irregular that they could not be made useful." Confederate artillerymen at Petersburg ran short of friction primers but continued firing their mortars by heating priming wires red hot and inserting them in the vents.

Mortars were useful in siege situations, but were not always available to field armies. Therefore, artillerymen often improvised by using tree trunks for their mortar tubes. According to a Union report of the siege of Knoxville: "The repeated assaults upon this fort, and the close proximity of the enemy's rifle-pits, made it very desirable to mount two or three mortars for the purpose of shelling out the enemy's trenches. As none were on hand, a wooden mortar was constructed, capable of throwing a 24-pounder howitzer shell. It was made of a live white oak, $2\frac{1}{2}$ feet in diameter, and when finished, the thickness of the wood was 1 foot and in rear of the seat of the charge from 18 inches to 2 feet. It was hooped with three iron bands shrunk on, and mounted on a bed of oak. It was fired with a 24-pounder howitzer shell and 7 ounces of powder, and withstood the test admirably; but subsequently, being fired with the same projectile and 16 ounces of good powder, it burst in two."

NAVAL GUNS

Naval guns saw use not only on ships, but on seacoast defense fortifications on land, operated sometimes by naval crews and at other times by army heavy artillerymen.

The Union Navy was blessed with the ordnance creativity of Rear Admiral John A. Dahlgren, chief of Naval Ordnance from July, 1862, to June, 1863, when he assumed a sea command. His first heavy iron gun design was submitted in 1850, and a 9-inch smoothbore was cast to his design at the West Point Foundry. The 9-inch tube, which weighed

9,000 pounds, was successfully tested and led to its production in 10- and 11-inch (weighing 15,700 pounds) calibers as well. The weapon was designed specifically to fire shells into wooden vessels, but it was so strong that it was also capable of dealing with the increased charges fired into ironclads. In practice, the U.S. Navy used the 9-inch guns, which fired 70-pound shot, on broadsides, and the 11-inch guns, which fired 127-pound shot, for its pivot guns. The Dahlgren gun had an especially modern, smooth shape, leading British ordnance experts to dub them "soda-water bottles."

Dahlgren also designed 15- and 20-inch naval guns in 1862. These were cast at the Fort Pitt Foundry using the Rodman system of cooling them from the inside. These tubes were lighter than the true Rodman guns, weighing 42,000 pounds as opposed to some 50,000 for the Rodmans. Their maximum diameter was 48 inches, and the bore length was 130 inches. They could fire solid shot weighing 440 pounds, cored shot weighing 400 pounds, shells weighing 330 pounds, grape, or canister.

In 1864, the Navy had a 20-inch gun cast to Dahlgren's design. It was 204 inches long with a bore 163 inches long. Its maximum diameter was 64 inches, and total weight of about 100,000 pounds. It would fire a 1,000-pound cored shot, taking a 100-pound standard charge. It apparently saw only experimental use, in which it was successful in breaking through the toughest iron plate available.

The Navy also ordered several 13-inch Dahlgren guns, which were cast in the standard manner, but they proved a failure, each exploding after only firing several rounds of solid shot. Versions cast in the Rodman style successfully fired over 500 cored shot rounds in experiments, but they were never put into production, the 15-inch being ordered for Monitor-class boats instead.

Additionally, some 10-inch Dahlgren guns were cast, as were 50- and 80-pounders. The 50-pounder first appeared in late 1861, while the 80-pounder appeared in the middle of that year. The 80-pounders exhibited an alarming tendency to burst when firing, and were soon replaced. The log of the U.S.S. *Hetzel* noted, on February 7, 1862: "At 5:15, rifled 80-pounder aft, loaded with 6 pounds powder and solid Dahlgren shot, 80 pounds, burst in the act of firing into four principal pieces. The gun forward of the trunnions fell on deck. One third of the breech passed over the mastheads and fell clear of the ship on the starboard bow. One struck on port quarter. And the fourth piece, weighing about 1,000 pounds, driving through the deck and

The largest gun cast in the world to that date was this 20-inch Rodman gun mounted at Fort Hamilton, New York. It was fired only four times during the war. (Library of Congress)

magazine, bringing up on the keelson, set fire to the ship." A handful of 150-pounders were also produced, but their quality was distrusted, and they never saw actual service.

Dahlgren himself was concerned about the safety of such large weapons, and ordered their use limited to fire against ironclads, and then with reduced charges. In action, in the turret of the U.S.S. *Weehawken*, a Monitor-class ship, a 15-inch Dahlgren/Rodman gun, firing at full charge behind a 400-pound cored shot, smashed through the armor of the C.S.S. *Atlanta* at 300 yards. Although the *Weehawken* needed to fire only five rounds, with both its 15- and 11-inch guns, the *Atlanta*, having run aground and being unable to bring its guns to bear, was forced to surrender due to the damage done by the large gun. These 15-inch guns, called Rodmans by the army and Dahlgrens by the navy, were also acquired by the army for its forts around Washington and along the seacoast.

Loading a 15-inch Rodman gun at Fort Monroe, Virginia. Note that a hoist is used to bring the solid shot to the muzzle, due to the heavy weight of the shot. (National Archives)

The Union Navy also used 6.4-inch and 8-inch Parrott rifles that were essentially the same as the army models.

The Confederates came up with one unique piece of heavy rifled artillery of their own, the Brooke rifle. It was designed by a Confederate Navy officer, John M. Brooke, Chief of the Bureau of Ordnance and Hydrography. It was a cast-iron gun using wrought-iron reinforcing bands around the breech. Different versions had different numbers of bands, ranging from one to three, with two being used on 7-inch to 10-inch guns. Rifling was similar to that of the British-made Blakely rifle, although Tredegar did cast one 7-inch Brooke that they did not rifle or band. In 1862, Tredegar also cast a 7-inch Brooke rifle which it triple banded.

A 7-inch Brooke rifle could send a projectile more than four and a half miles. Many of these weapons were made at Richmond's Tredegar Iron Works, which produced 14 of them between September, 1861, and March, 1862. Their sizes were recorded at 6.4-inch, 7-inch, 8-inch, 10-inch, and 11-inch. Tredegar also described several Brooke rifles that they cast as "32-pounders."

The largest source of Brooke guns, however, was the Confederate Navy itself. It set up its own naval gun foundry in Selma, Alabama, in 1863, casting its first 7-inch Brooke rifle in July, 1863. This gun was not acceptable, and the foundry furnaces were rebuilt. Its next guns were also failures, for various reasons, but by January, 1864, the foundry was able to supply its first 7-inch Brooke rifle to the C.S.S. *Tennessee*. Other Selma-cast Brooke rifles went to land fortifications, such as the defenses of Mobile, Alabama. The foundry also cast 10-inch and 11-inch Brooke guns for harbor defense. Selma-produced Brookes in 6.4- and 7-inch were rifled, while the 8-, 10-, and 11-inch Brookes were smoothbores. All told, the foundry produced 102 Brooke rifles and guns.

The Brooke turned out to be a very serviceable design, although prone to bursting more through manufacturing flaws than design flaws. On January 9, 1864, General P.G.T. Beauregard wrote Colonel Josiah Gorgas, Chief of Ordnance, the results of experiments in ordnance tried at Charleston, where he commanded: "Gen. Ripley, in one of his reports, makes the following statement:

"The Brooke gun at Fort Sumter was fired with 15 pounds of powder at 18 degrees elevation, and although the charge was less than the maximum it finally cracked through the vent, and the gun was condemned. Happening to be present I ordered a reduction in using the remaining gun of the same kind, and better ranges were obtained with 10 pounds of mixed coarse-grained and common cannon powder.

"With $20\frac{1}{2}$ degrees a shell of 100 pounds was thrown 4 miles into the enemy's camp, and with 23 degrees it was thrown beyond Light-House Inlet and on Folly Island."

Major-General Dabney Maury, in writing of the defense of Mobile, noted: "But we had some cannon better than any Parrott had ever made. They were the Brooke guns, made at Selma in the Confederate naval works of the iron from Briarsfield, Alabama the best iron for making cannon in the world.

"Our Brooke guns at Mobile were rifles, of 11 inch, 10 inch, 7 inch and $6\frac{4}{10}$ inch calibers. They outranged the Parrotts, and, though subjected to extraordinary service, not one of them was ever bursted or even strained."

Even so, as with all big guns, Brookes were not immune to premature explosions if incorrectly used. Colonel William Lamb, commander of Fort Fisher, wrote that during the final attack on his fort: "My two seven-inch Brooke rifles both exploded in the afternoon of this day. Being manned by a detachment of sailors and situated opposite to the bar, I had given the officer in charge discretion to fire upon the vessels which had approached the bar, and his fire had been more rapid than from any other guns, and with the disastrous result of explosion, which unfortunately wounded a number of men."

An experimental carriage for a Rodman gun tested at Fort Monroe, Virginia. The idea was to make for easy and accurate elevation. The system was never adopted. (Library of Congress)

Major Manigault noted on September 19, 1863: "Commended firing … with 4.62 in. Rifle No. 1. Fired 7 Shots with good effect when the rear Band of the piece showed symptoms of Starting from the one in front of it and the black, semi-liquid unctuous residuum from inflamed gunpowder oozed out from between the bands. Ceased firing from this gun, which must now be regarded as positively dangerous, and unfit for use. (Total Number of Shots fired from it by us 261, at an average elevation of 13 $\frac{1}{2}$ degrees, 4 lbs of Powder, and Average Weight of projecting probably 27 or 28 lbs.) The Vent is very much enlarged and quite ragged." This weapon, judging from the description of the "bands" was probably a Brooke rifle.

A Parrott rifle, front, and a Rodman gun, behind it, in Battery Rodgers, overlooking the Potomac River in Alexandria, Virginia. (Library of Congress)

BRITISH-MADE GUNS

Great Britain made the most advanced artillery available in 1861 and the Confederates, since they were unable to make as many guns as they needed for themselves, took advantage of British technology by buying as many guns as possible from overseas. Early in the war, the Confederate War Department sent Caleb Huse as its purchasing agent to London.

On the subject of British-made heavy artillery, Huse wrote the War Department in Richmond on May 21, 1861: "I have in my possession detailed drawings of the Armstrong gun, which I shall copy and forward by the first opportunity. I shall also be able to send with these full descriptions of the mode of manufacture, as given by Sir William [G. Armstrong] himself, and drawings of his fuse … There seems to be no doubt, however, from the inquiries I have made, that the British Government has entire confidence in the Armstrong gun. To the large guns there appears to be some objection."

Furthermore, he wrote: "I have met Capt. Blakely and have conversed with him about his gun. As yet I have failed to see anything in his principle which would cause me to purchase his cannon. He uses the same principle that Armstrong employs of wrapping an interior core with wrought-iron spirals and in fact he claims the merit of the invention. The chief difference appears to be that Capt. Blakely uses a cast-iron core, while Sir William has a wrought-iron centerpiece. The Northern States have purchased some Clay breech-loaders, I am informed, at enormous prices. From the accounts I have received of them, and from a cursory inspection of one, I should think the men about the breech would stand a little better chance than the enemy, but that the difference would be very slight. I am told that they were invoiced as Armstrong guns. The true Armstrong cannot be had. I think, however, that they can be manufactured from the drawings which I shall send to the Department."

Confederate ordnance officers were told that Clay wanted £400 [$2,000] for an 8-inch gun and £500 [$2,500] for a 9-inch and, despite the cost, ordered at least one for testing. Recalled E. Porter Alexander: "A few of the favorite English rifled guns were brought through the

A 20-pounder Parrott rifle, the smallest piece of artillery considered "heavy artillery." (Gettysburg National Battlefield Park)

blockade, and used in the Army of Northern Virginia, comprising the Clay, Whitworth, Blakely, and Armstrong shunt pattern. The Clay gun was a breech-loader, and was called an improvement upon the breech-loading Armstrong, which was manufactured for the English Government only, and could not be obtained. Its grooving and its breech-loading arrangements appeared simpler and of greater strength. On trial, however, it failed in every particular. Every projectile fired 'tumbled' and fell nearer the gun than the target, and at the seventh round the solid breech piece was cracked through and the gun disabled."

That left the Blakely and the Armstrong, which was not available since the British Government had an interest in Armstrong's company until 1862. Thereafter, his guns became available to the South. Charleston citizen Joseph Walker wrote on October 24, 1863, to Charleston's commander, General P.G.T. Beauregard: "During my recent visit to Europe, from where I have just returned … I gained some information about guns, in my investigation, that I thought might be of some importance, and have transmitted the facts to Col. Gorgas, at Richmond.

"The main facts are these: That ten guns of 9-inch and ten guns of 11- inch cast-steel, of the Blakely pattern, can be had immediately. They are a good gun, and will penetrate two plates, each of 4 inches thickness.

"Second: That the Armstrong gun can be gotten, through a friend, in any number. Sir William Armstrong does not wish his name to appear, in consequence of his relations to his own Government."

In fact, the Confederates purchased both weapons, two Blakely rifles arriving in Charleston in September, 1863. Colonel William Lamb, commander of Fort Fisher, described his North Carolina post: "The land face mounted twenty of the heaviest seacoast guns, and was 682 yards long; the sea face with twenty-four equally heavy guns (including a 170-pounder Blakely rifle and 130-pounder Armstrong rifle, both imported from England) was 1,898 yards in length."

The Armstrong was produced from wrought-iron tubes made from spiral coils welded into a single bar as bands formed around a mandrel. Steel replaced wrought-iron for the main tube by the end of 1864, although the rest of the weapon was made of these bands formed around the mandrel. Additionally, the first Armstrong guns were breech-loaders, but these failed, and after early 1863 the company made all its guns as muzzle-loaders. The weapons were "shunt rifles," a process that used a small number of grooves in the barrel and ammunition with matching rows of zinc strips (later brass studs) to engage the grooves. The 150-pounder Armstrong rifle used at Fort Fisher was a breech-loader mounted on a British barbette carriage that featured six traverse wheels and side compressors, something not seen on American-made carriages.

Blakely guns were made of cast iron with wrought iron or, more commonly, steel breech bands. They were produced by various British makers, including Fawcett, Preston & Co.; Low Moor Iron Co.; George Forrester & Co.; and Blakely Ordnance Co., and sold to various foreign powers, including Russia, and to Massachusetts, which bought eight 9-inch and four 11-inch models during the war. The 9-inch fired a 248-pound bolt, using a 30-pound charge. The 11-inch fired a 375-pound bolt with a 37.25 pound charge. A 4.5-inch version was used at Fort Pulaski, while 7.5-inch versions were used by the Confederates at Vicksburg and in northern Virginia. Two 8-inch, 200-pounder Blakelys were in the defenses of Mobile, Alabama, while the two Charleston guns were 12.75-inch. The latter were the largest rifled guns in the Confederate arsenal.

Major Edward Manigualt reported from the defenses of Charleston in September 1863, that his crew, "Fired also 4 Shell with the 4 in. Blakely Gun. The results were unsatisfactory. The projectiles flew very wildly. Elevations 13°, 14°, 15° & 16 $\frac{1}{2}$°." Again, on September 21, he wrote: "In afternoon fired 6 Shots with 4 inch Blakely gun at Black Island. The results very unsatisfactory. We can make nothing of this gun with the projectiles furnished us."

Even so, Charleston's defenders wanted even bigger Blakely guns, and ordered two 12.75-inch Blakely guns for that post. Made of cast iron with a bronze air chamber at the breech, with a steel band around the powder chamber, they weighed almost 50,000 pounds each and each special carriage with all accessories weighed 58,000 pounds. Each solid cylindrical shot was 20 inches long and weighed 650 pounds. The powder charge for the bolt was 50 pounds and shells weighed 470 pounds. Due to their weight, the weapon had a small hoist on the top of the barrel that allowed the shot to be raised to the muzzle. The gun used a huge four-wheeled top carriage that allowed the weapon to be loaded, and then moved up the bottom carriage into firing position. The recoil shoved the top carriage back after firing. Sliding friction against the bottom carriage reduced strain on carriage and gun.

Once loaded, the charge was rammed against the reinforced breech, but not into the bronze chamber which was to remain free to serve as an air-filled shock absorber. Then a projectile was placed in the lifting mechanism and cranked to the muzzle. The shell or bolt flanges had to be aligned to the rifling by hand and then the shot was rammed in until snug against the cartridge. The gun would then be moved forward, aimed with two vertical gunsights and a

Parrott rifles at Battery Meade, Morris Island, during the firing into Charleston. (Library of Congress)

A: The 24-pounder siege gun and carriage

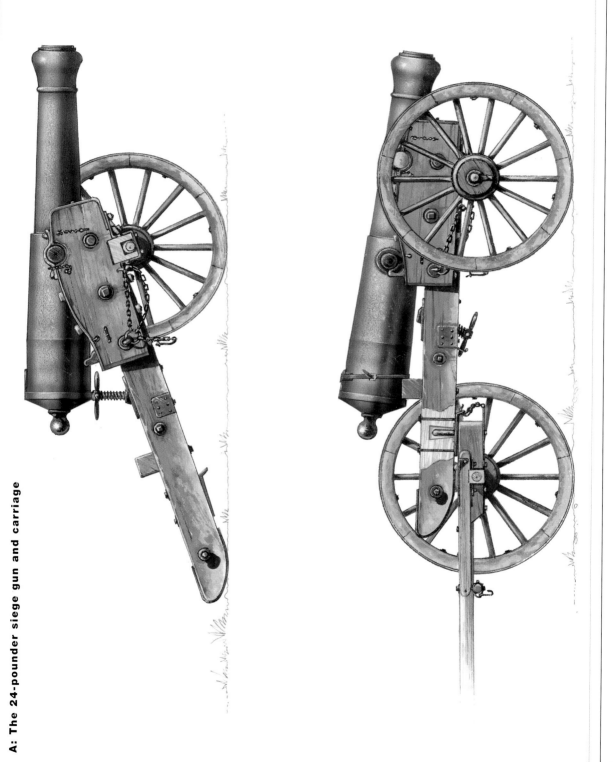

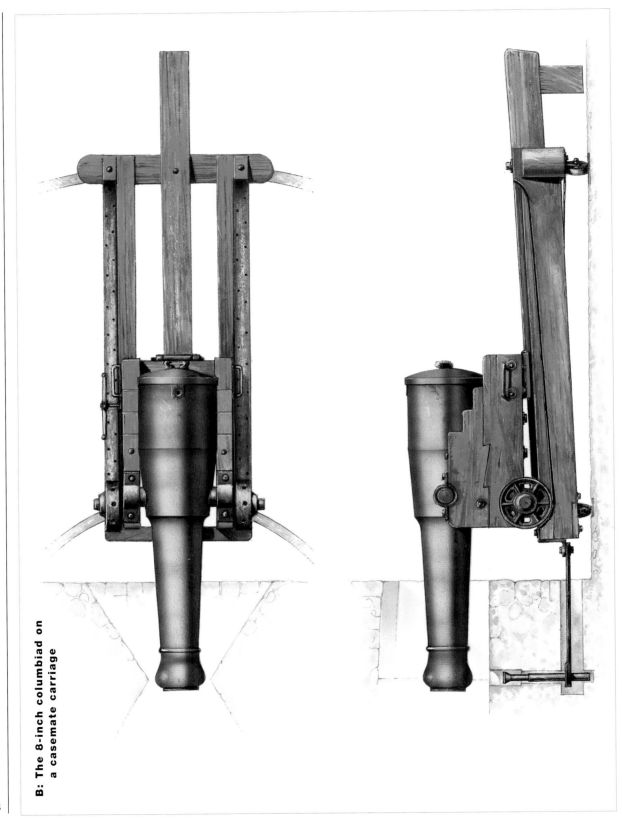

B: The 8-inch columbiad on a casemate carriage

B

C: A typical seacoast prewar fortification

c

100-PDR. PARROT RIFLE ON IRON CASEMATE CARRIAGE

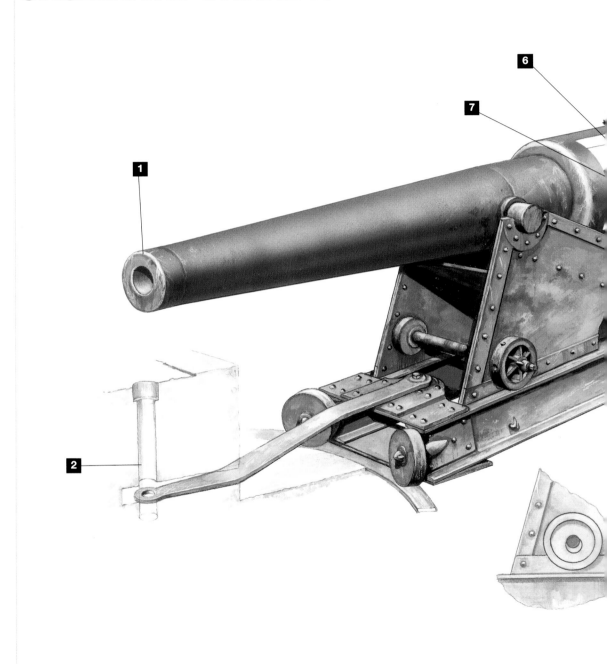

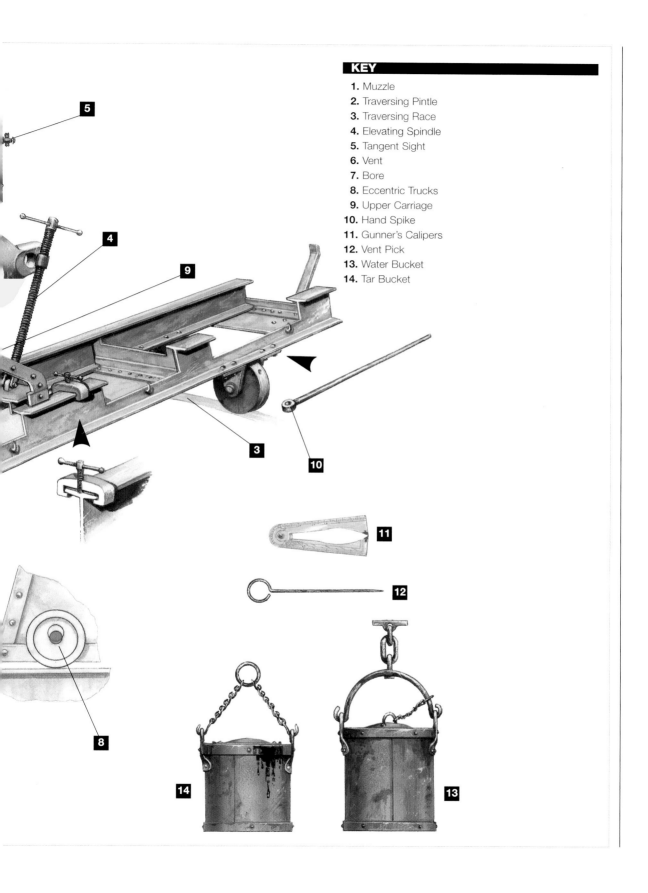

E: A 150-pounder Armstrong, top, and a 13-inch siege mortar and carriage, bottom

F: The fortifications of Vicksburg

F

G: Ammunition

A

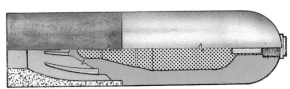

E

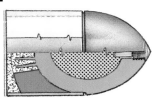

B

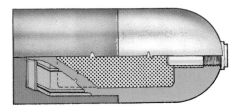

F

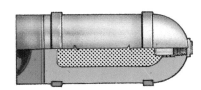

C

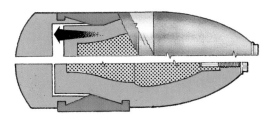

G

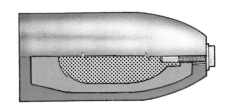

D

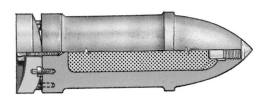

H

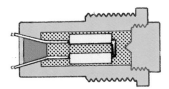

A Parrott rifle in the fortifications around Fort Stevens, Washington, DC, where President Abraham Lincoln actually came under fire during the Confederate raid on the city in 1864.

screw jack. A pointer on the right trunnion indicated the degrees of elevation. Then the lanyard was pulled and the weapon fired. Loading and firing was a slow operation.

Placed in position, the Charleston guns were tested before artillerymen received the necessary instruction manual. The novice gunners, not understanding the purpose of the air chamber behind the breech, loaded three charges into the air chamber and another in the breech. The incorrect loading ruptured the chamber, cracking the cast-iron breech in 11 places. Confederate ordnance reported on October 3, 1863: "The bursting of the heavy rifled guns is not sufficiently explained by the character of the metal, as Gen. Beauregard supposes. The cast iron of these guns was entirely satisfactory, and their premature destruction is due to the constant heavy charges with which they have been fired. But the same excuse cannot be made for the bursting of the 600-pounder imported Blakely gun. The destruction of this formidable gun was due to a want of forethought, unpardonable in an officer as experienced as Gen. Ripley, as appears from the following telegram, just received from Capt. Harding (October 3), as to remaining gun:

"Col. Yates yesterday fired large Blakely gun with charges from 30 to 55 pounds powder, 470 pound shell, with perfect success; elevation, 2 degrees; gave range 1 1/4 miles; cartridge in front of brass chamber." Thus the second gun, correctly loaded, proved a success. Local mechanics repaired the breech of the first gun and got that back into service.

The Confederates also purchased one other type of British-made rifle, the Whitworth 70-pounder (5-inch), as well as smaller 12-pounders (2.75-inch), some of which ended up in fortifications such as Fort Fisher. Several of these 70-pounders were later captured by Union blockaders, and then used against the Confederates around Charleston. Confederate E. Porter Alexander recalled in 1866 that Whitworths "often rendered valuable service by their great range and accuracy. They fired solid shot almost exclusively; but they were perfectly reliable, and their projectiles never failed to fly in the most beautiful trajectory imaginable. Their breech-loading arrangements, however, often worked with difficulty…" Union experts around Charleston, however, disliked the 70-pounders, finding them prone to premature explosions when firing shell, difficult to operate since the projectile tended to wedge halfway into the breech, and inaccurate compared to 8-inch Parrotts.

Confederates generally held their British-made, breech-loading guns in reserve, because of the cost of the ammunition. As Fort Fisher's Colonel Lamb recalled: "The Armstrong gun had only one dozen rounds of fixed ammunition, and no other projectile could be used in its delicate groves." However, when they were fired, they proved worth their cost. In reporting on a Union assault on Fort Fisher, North Carolina, Lamb noted: "About 2 p.m. the flagship and other frigates came closer to the bar and lowered boats, which approached to sound the bar. The Brooke gun battery opened upon them, with other guns, and drove them out. The Armstrong gun, which had been held in reserve during the fight, was pointed late in the afternoon on the flagship lying off the bar, and one steel shot amidships caused the admiral's pennant again to withdraw."

Nonetheless, all the British-made rifles presented problems because they required ammunition beyond Southern manufacturing capabilities. As Alexander recalled: "The Blakely guns were twelve pounder rifles, muzzle loaders, and fired very well with English ammunition ('built up' shells with leaden bases), but with the Confederate substitute, they experienced the same difficulties which attended this ammunition in all guns."

Parrott rifles at Fort Brady, one of the ring of forts around Washington, DC, manned by members of Co. G, 1st Connecticut Heavy Artillery. (Library of Congress)

AMMUNITION

A brief examination of period heavy-artillery ammunition alone could more than fill a book this size. Basically, period ammunition included solid shot, shells, canister, and grape. Shells came in a variety of styles, including shells that had a brass, iron, copper, or lead cap or ring attached to their base (Parrott, Absterdam, Read, Cochran, Dimick, Mullane, Burton and Archer, Harding); shells with lead or paper around the outside that squeezed into the grooves on firing (Schenkl, Dyer, James); shells that were shaped to fit a specific bore (Whitworth, Armstrong); shells with projections that fit into the bore grooves (Sawyer, Blakely, Pattison, Dahlgren); and shells with a soft metal covering that was driven into the grooves on firing (Sawyer, Hotchkiss, Burton). The Confederates also produced a winged shot that came with slotted wings that sprang open on leaving the muzzle in an attempt to obtain rifled accuracy with smoothbore guns.

For anti-personnel use, siege guns used grapeshot, which had been replaced by canister for field artillery use. According to Colonel Scott, grapeshot consisted of: "a certain number of cast-iron balls put together by means of two cast-iron plates, two rings, and one pin and nut." Grapeshot provided to 8-inch guns was made up of 6-pounder shot.

One of the largest Parrott rifles ever made was nicknamed "the Swamp Angel" and was placed to fire into Charleston. It burst after only a few rounds, the men having taken months to get the ground in the swampy area hard enough to stand the weight of the gun. (Library of Congress)

Cored shot, as used in some naval guns as well as Parrotts, was designed to be used against masonry forts. Some Parrott shells were filled with six pints of Berney's incendiary composition, a mixture of turpentine and petroleum, or a pint of Flemming's composition. This ammunition was designed to set wooden buildings alight upon exploding.

Northern-made Stafford armor-piercing ammunition was designed for use against ironclads. It featured a steel bolt cased in wood with a brass sabot at the rear. The bolt would drive through the armor, while the wood casing would fall apart on the face of the armor. These came in 6.4-inch and 8-inch sizes.

Southern-made ammunition was universally condemned, save, perhaps, by its targets. Confederate Major Edward Manigault noted on August 29, 1863: "After a good many shots found that the 24 pndr. Rifle could not be relied on at that distance with the new shell furnished us. The Shells made by J.M. Easton & Co. (a Charleston machine shop and foundry) according to a pattern which was furnished with the original Blakely Gun sent to this country (Prioleau Gun) reached Morris Island, but they have all been expended and the other shells furnished cannot be relied on at all and have all fallen short. [This Blakely gun was presented to South Carolina by Charles K. Prioleau of Frazer & Co. in 1861.]"

A Parrott rifle mounted on a well-defended railroad car during the siege of Petersburg. (Library of Congress)

Manigault wrote again on September 8, 1863: 'I have to complain of the character of the Rifle projectiles lately furnished me. As for instance, Solid Conical Shot for 4.62-in. Gun, weighing 40 lbs. = $3\frac{1}{2}$ times the weight of Spherical projectiles of same caliber. Shell for 24-pndr Rifle (5.82-in. Cal.) weighing 60 lbs. = $2\frac{1}{2}$ times weight of solid spherical shot of same Caliber. Solid Conical Shot of 80 lbs weight - 3 $\frac{1}{2}$ times weight of solid Spherical shot of Same diameter. And this last for a gun not originally intended as a Rifle, but simply converted by Rifling & Banding. Not only will the guns be enormously strained by these projectiles fired at high Elevations and soon burst, but also, with smaller charges than 10 lbs. & 5 lbs. of powder, respectively for the 5.82- and 4.62-in. Calibers, the Range will not be great. If great penetration were required at distances of from half a mile to 1 mile then these heavy solid shot might be suitable, but They are entirely unsuitable for a Range of 2 $\frac{1}{2}$ miles, which is required for Morris Island (at least without increasing the Charge of Powder to an extent extremely dangerous with any guns we have)."

The Navy mounted 100-pounder Parrotts such as this one on the U.S.S. *Mendota*. (U.S. Army Military History Institute)

The damage done by both shells and solid shot depended largely on where they landed. Soft soil and sand, for example, would absorb the shell and most of its power would be lost, while hard soil would allow the shell to explode all around and shot to ricochet. Major Frederick Shonnard, 6th New York Heavy Artillery, wrote after watching a mortar shell land in sandy soil at the feet of one of his men: "A soldier was walking in towards me from the picket line, suddenly as I looked at him a shell dropped right at his feet burying itself in the sandy soil, in another instant the shell exploded and lifted him off the ground. Calling some of my men to follow, I jumped over our work and ran to him. To my amazement I was unable to lift him; the explosion had forced sand into and under his clothing so that he was as heavy as if made of stone. Men coming up opened his clothing and relieved him of sand sufficiently so that they could carry him. He was unconscious but finally when he regained his senses it was made plain that he was not hurt in any way. The shell had buried itself in the deep sandy soil before exploding."

Forts that guarded the seacoasts were provided with furnaces for heating shot to be fired into wooden ships so that they would catch fire. Each furnace was designed to hold 60 or more shot. When users put shot into a cold furnace and started its fires, it would take an hour and a quarter to heat shot red hot. After the furnace was heated, a 24-pounder shot could be heated red hot in 25 minutes, while 32-pounder and 42-pounder shot took only a few minutes longer. It took a crew of two to three men to keep a furnace going and put cold shot in and take hot shot out during normal operations. One man took out the shot hot and placed them on a stand to be scraped; another scraped them and put them into a ladle for carrying them to each gun, while the third supplied cold shot and fuel to the furnace.

Tripods were used to mount 100-pounder Parrotts on their carriages. (Library of Congress)

A wadding of either pure clay, fuller's earth, or wet hay was rammed between the charge and the hot shot to prevent premature explosions. According to period experiments, a red-hot shot retained enough heat to set wood alight even after ricocheting off the water a couple of times. After hitting the ship, the shot worked best if it penetrated only ten to 12 inches, because a ball that went deeper could not get enough air to flame the embers. Therefore, ordnance officers advised using only a quarter to a sixth charge when firing hot shot the same distance as one would use to fire cold shot.

Cannonballs themselves were actually placed in piles near their guns. According to the ordnance manual, "Balls are piled according to kind and caliber, under cover if practicable, in a place where there is a free circulation of air, to facilitate which, the piles should be made narrow if the locality permits; the width of the bottom tier may be from 12 to 14 balls, according to the caliber." So that gunners could quickly identify the correct ammunition to use, solid shot for 8-inch guns and all spherical case shot were painted red, while all other cannonballs were painted black. Grape and canister shot were either oiled or painted and stored either in piles or in strong boxes marked with the contents.

HEAVY ARTILLERY USAGE

The main purpose of heavy artillery was to defend and attack fixed fortifications. These fortifications were made of brick, stone, and mortar along the coast and, where newer fortifications were especially created to match the occasion as at around Washington or Richmond, of earth and sand bags. In fact, the newer fortifications did better under fire from the heavy guns then available.

The siege of Fort Pulaski, Georgia, was a test of all types of heavy artillery of the period. The fort, defending the approach to Savannah along a river leading into the city, was a single-story pentagon-shaped brickwork with a line of guns inside and a line *en barbette* (meaning exposed on the top of the fort's walls). Its construction had begun in 1829 and by 1847 it could be said to be only "nearly complete." Essentially it, as were the other fortifications along America's seacoast, had been designed to withstand smoothbore artillery of the Napoleonic era. Its armament was to consist of 150 guns, none larger than a 32-pounder, of which there were 65, and which was still the heaviest gun in its garrison in 1860. By November, 1862, it had, *en barbette*, five 10-inch columbiads, six 8-inch columbiads, and two 10-inch mortars. The casements contained three 8-inch columbiads, two 42-pounder guns, 20 32-pounder guns, and one 24-pounder gun. Later, the Confederates were able to add imported British-made Blakely 24-pounder rifled guns to this garrison.

In May, 1861, British correspondent Lord Russell visited the post, which he thought was ill-suited for the day, noting that the Confederates "do not understand the nature of the new shell and heavy vertical fire, or the effect of projectiles from great distances falling into open works." The Confederates, however, felt that no siege artillery could smash through the fort's brick walls from the distances at which they would have to be placed.

The Union forces planned to take Fort Pulaski, the main defense of Savannah, as an entrance into Georgia. The chief engineer planning the siege called for a force of ten 10-inch mortars, ten 13-inch mortars, eight heavy rifled guns, and eight columbiads. These were to be placed in batteries ranging from 2,600 yards to 3,700 yards from the fort. In fact, 36 Union guns were to take part in this siege. These were placed as follows: three heavy 13-inch mortars at 3,400 yards from the fort; three heavy 13-inch mortars 3,200 yards away; three heavy 10-inch columbiads 3,100 yards away; three heavy 8-inch mortars 3,045 yards away; one heavy 13-inch mortar 2,750 yards away; three heavy 13-inch mortars 2,650 yards away; two heavy 13-inch mortars 2,400 yards away; three 10-inch columbiads and one 8-inch columbiad 1,740 yards away; five 30-pounder Parrotts and one 48-pounder James rifle, which had been rebored from a 24-pounder, 1,670 yards away; two 84-pounder James rifles, rebored from 42-pounder smoothbores, and two 64-pounder James rifles, rebored from 32-pounder smoothbores, 1,650 yards away; and four 10-inch siege mortars 1,650 yards away.

On April 10, 1862, the Union forces opened fire on the fort. At first the Union shelling seemed to their observers to have little effect. Confederate return fire was also ineffective, most of the shells falling short into the river or sinking into the marshes and exploding uselessly. Inside the fort, however, things were not going well at all. The rifled shells, particularly from the James rifles, blasted brick dust everywhere. Within three hours, three casement guns were disabled. That evening, the Confederate commander examined his post and found, "It was worse than disheartening, the pan-coupe at the southeast angle was entirely breached while above, on the rampart, the parapet had been shot away and an 8-inch gun, the muzzle of which was gone, hung trembling over the verge. The two adjacent casemates were rapidly approaching the same ruined condition; masses of broken masonry nearly filled the moat, as was the interior of the three casemates where the dismounted guns lay like logs among the bricks."

The Parrott guns were concentrated on exposed Confederate guns, and it was later seen

Large Parrott rifles were prone to premature explosions which could hurl heavy chunks of metal some distance, such as on this gun photographed in the Union lines besieging Charleston, South Carolina.

The muzzle was blown off this 300-pounder Parrott rifle in Battery Strong, part of the ring of Union force facing Charleston. It exploded on its 27th round, losing some 20 inches of tube. The tube was then cut down and fired another 371 rounds before more cracks around the muzzle forced the gun's retirement.

The Union position at Crow's Nest at Dutch Gap, during the Petersburg campaign, is outfitted with 10-inch mortars. (Library of Congress)

that 10 percent of Parrott projectiles tumbled end over end.

Firing continued through the night and into the next day, and by late morning the Union observers noted that several casemates had been entirely opened, in a hole big enough for a two-horse wagon, and the moat had been almost filled with bricks, masonry, and gun parts. By the end of the day, it was clear that defense was impossible, and the Confederates surrendered. The Union guns had been firing continuously for 18 hours before the surrender.

During the two-day bombardment, Union forces fired 1,394 shot and 3,923 shells for a total of 5,317 rounds. In all, 1,732 were mortar rounds, 1,250 were fired from columbiads, 1,024 were James rounds, and 1,311 were fired from the Parrotts. Close examination showed that a single 84-pounder James shell, fired at $4\frac{1}{2}°$ with an 8-pound charge, penetrated 26 inches of masonry. A 30-pounder Parrott shot penetrated 18 inches. A 128-pound solid shot from a 10-inch columbiad penetrated 13 inches; a 68-pound shot from an 8-inch columbiad penetrated 11 inches. A 42-pounder shot dug up to 12 feet into the earthen traverses between the guns *en barbette*. In all, 58 percent of the shot that penetrated the fort's walls was fired by rifled guns, with the rest from smoothbores. The result was a breach 30 feet wide with an adjacent scarp wall that was severely damaged across three casemates. In all, 110,643 pounds of metal had been fired at this point to do so much damage.

Clearly, rifled pieces did the most damage, and most observers felt that they won the day. The smoothbore contribution was relatively small, and had the besieging force had only columbiads and mortars, the siege would have gone on a great deal longer. The chief engineer at the siege calculated that heavy smoothbore guns would have been effective if closer than 700 yards from the fort, but beyond that range rifled guns were vastly better in breaching masonry walls. According to him: "… good rifled guns, properly served, can breach rapidly at 1,650 yards distance. A few heavy round shot, to bring down the masses loosened by the rifled projectiles, are of good service."

Mortars were of little value. Only 10 percent of their shells fell within the fort's walls. Their only real value was in silencing the guns *en barbette* and setting alight wooden buildings inside the fort. One mortar dug a hole seven feet deep on the fort's parade ground.

Confederate counterbattery fire had been totally ineffective, even before most of their guns were disabled.

The era of fortifications that had lasted from the days of Vaubaun were gone. A Union visitor after the surrender reported that rifled "steel pointed shot bored through the brick walls as if they were so much paper." Old-fashioned forts were suddenly obsolete, due to modern heavy artillery, and, "We must have iron forts and ironclad ships."

U.S. ARMY ORGANIZATION

Heavy artillery commands were organized largely along the same line as infantry regiments and battalions. According to an act of Congress passed in August, 1861: "Each regiment of infantry shall have one colonel, one lieutenant-colonel, one major, one adjutant (a lieutenant), one quartermaster (a lieutenant), one surgeon and one assistant surgeon, one sergeant-major, one regimental quartermaster-sergeant, one regimental commissary-sergeant, one hospital steward, two principal musicians, and twenty-four musicians for a band; and shall be composed of ten companies, each company to consist of one captain, one first lieutenant, one second lieutenant, one first sergeant, four sergeants, eight corporals, two musicians, one wagoner, and from sixty-four to eighty-two privates." A chaplain was also authorized.

Heavy artillery companies required more specialized men, such as blacksmiths, so these regiments were larger than infantry regiments. According to Major Frederick Shonnard, 6th New York Heavy Artillery, "An infantry regiment was comprised of ten companies of 100 men each, while an Artillery regiment was composed of twelve companies of 150 men each, each company being called a Battery. Such an organization could be used entirely as Infantry, divided into three battalions of six hundred men each, or partly as infantry."

The Provost Marshal-General's office sent this message, on April 20, 1864, to each of the state governors: 'The Secretary of War has ordered that new regiments of heavy artillery that may be organized and filled up to the legal standard of 1,738 men, within the period of twenty days from this date, will be received and credited. If regiments are not full on or before the 10th of May the recruits will be put into other artillery or infantry organizations." At this point, the government would rather have had infantry than heavy artillery regiments.

Even so, the same basic 1861 company organization remained. On April 15, 1863, the XVI Corps issued orders for eight heavy artillery companies to garrison Fort Pickering.

Battery No. 4, one of 15 batteries planted to the south and southeast of Yorktown for McClellan's superfluous siege, contained ten 13-inch siege mortars. (Library of Congress)

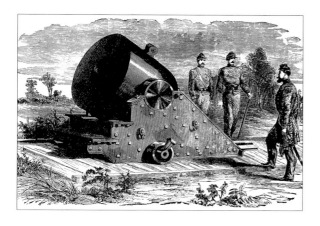

A 13-inch mortar, weighing 17,000 pounds, as shown on the pages of *Frank Leslie's Illustrated News*.

They read:

"I. Pursuant to orders from the Secretary of War (Brig. Gen. L. Thomas, Adjutant-Gen. U. S. Army) there will be recruited and mustered into the service of the United States eight companies of colored men for service as heavy artillery at Fort Pickering.

"II. The recruiting, organization, and examination of recruits will be as directed by regulations.

"III. Each company will have one captain, two lieutenants, and an orderly-sergeant, who will be white; the other noncommissioned officers will be from the colored recruits."

The following units were raised as regiments of heavy artillery for the U.S. Army: 1st Connecticut Regiment, 2d Connecticut Regiment, Ahl's Delaware Company, 1st Indiana Regiment, 1st Louisiana Siege Artillery Regiment (African Descent), 1st Maine Regiment, Maine Garrison Artillery, 1st Massachusetts Regiment, 1st Massachusetts Battalion, 2d Massachusetts Regiment, 3d Massachusetts Regiment, 4th Massachusetts Regiment, 130 Massachusetts Companies, 6th Michigan Regiment, 1st Minnesota Regiment, and the 1st New Hampshire Regiment.

From New York: the 2d New York Regiment, 3d New York German Battalion, 4th New York Regiment, 4th New York National Guard, 4th New York Battalion (1st Black River Artillery Battalion), 5th New York Regiment (2d Jackson Regiment), 5th New York Battalion (2d Black River Artillery Battalion), 6th New York Regiment (Anthony Wayne Guard), 6th New York Battalion (3d Black River Artillery Battalion), 7th New York Regiment (Albany County Regiment/Seymour Guards), 7th New York Regiment (4th Black River Artillery Battalion), 8th New York Regiment, 9th New York Regiment (2d Auburn Regiment/Cayuga and Wayne County Regiment), 10th New York Regiment (Black River Artillery/Jefferson County Regiment), 11th New York Regiment. 13th New York Regiment, 12th New York State Militia, 14th New York Regiment, 15th New York Regiment, and the 16th New York Regiment.

A 13-inch mortar battery on Morris Island around the Union lines besieging Charleston.

From other states: the 1st North Carolina Regiment (African Descent), 1st Ohio Regiment, 2d Ohio Regiment, 2d Pennsylvania Regiment (112th Volunteers), 2d Pennsylvania Provisional Regiment, 3d Pennsylvania Regiment (152d Volunteers), 5th Pennsylvania Regiment (204th Volunteers), 6th Pennsylvania Regiment (212th Volunteers), Robert's Pennsylvania Battalion, Segebarth's Pennsylvania Marine Artillery Battalion, the Pennsylvania Commonwealth Company, Ermentrout's Pennsylvania Militia Company, Jones' Pennsylvania Independent Company, Schooley's Pennsylvania Independent Company, Tyler's Pennsylvania Company, and Woodward's Pennsylvania Company.

Also: the 3d Rhode Island Regiment, the 5th Rhode Island Regiment, the 14th Rhode Island Regiment, 1st Tennessee Regiment (African Descent), 2d Tennessee Regiment (African Descent), 1st Vermont Regiment, and 1st Wisconsin Regiment.

In the United States Army: Battery A, 1st Artillery; Battery C, 1st Artillery; Battery D, 1st Artillery; Battery H, 2d Artillery; Battery I, 2d Artillery; Battery K, 2d Artillery; Battery B, 3d Artillery; Battery D, 3d Artillery; Battery H, 3d Artillery; Battery D, 4th Artillery; Battery L, 4th Artillery; Battery G, 5th Artillery; 1st U.S. Colored Trooops (USCT), 3d USCT, 4th USCT, 5th USCT, 6th USCT, 7th USCT, 8th USCT, 9th USCT, 10th USCT, 11th USCT, 12th USCT, 13th USCT, and 14th USCT.

This 13-inch mortar was mounted on a railway car so as to be able to be fired from different places into the Confederate lines around Petersburg. (Library of Congress)

C.S. ORGANIZATION

Initially, heavy artillery was organized the same as infantry regiments or battalions. Each company, after November 1861, was set at a minimum of 70 men, with 10 companies in a regiment. This was raised to 150 men in a company as of October 11, 1862. A full regiment would rate a colonel, a lieutenant-colonel, a major, an adjutant who ranked as a lieutenant, a commissary who ranked as a captain, a quartermaster who ranked as a captain, a surgeon who ranked as a major, a sergeant-major, an ordnance sergeant, and a hospital steward. Each company would have a captain, a first lieutenant, a second lieutenant, an orderly or first sergeant, and a sufficient number of other noncommissioned officers.

On March 3, 1862, Adjutant & Inspector General Samuel Cooper wrote to the Secretary of War, Judah P. Benjamin, about a problem that arose from the small number of officers and NCOs in heavy artillery units: "The organization of these companies is the same as infantry, and some of them are assigned to batteries of from six to nine heavy guns. Each section of two pieces should be commanded by a lieutenant and each gun should be provided with a sergeant and corporal, so that a company serving a battery of eight guns should have four lieutenants, eight sergeants, and eight corporals; whereas at present organized the company consists of only three lieutenants, five sergeants, and four corporals." Benjamin agreed, sending the suggestion on to Congress, which also agreed, reorganizing heavy artillery to be the same as light artillery batteries on April 3, 1862.

The following Confederate units were specifically raised and served as heavy artillery units: 12th Georgia Artillery Battalion (Savannah Siege Train Heavy Artillery Battalion), 22d Georgia Artillery (Siege) Battalion, 28th Georgia Artillery Battalion, 1st Regular Louisiana Artillery Regiment, 2d Louisiana Artillery Battalion, 8th Louisiana Artillery Battalion, 1st Mississippi Artillery Regiment, 1st North Carolina Heavy Artillery Battalion, 3d North Carolina Artillery Battalion, 10th North Carolina Artillery Battalion (2d Battalion Heavy Artillery),

The Navy mounted 13-inch mortars on schooners to use to bombard shore points, such as Forts St Philip and Jackson outside New Orleans in 1862. (Library of Congress)

10th Regiment North Carolina Volunteers Artillery (five companies), 40th Regiment North Carolina Volunteers–3d Artillery, 1st South Carolina Heavy Artillery Regiment, 2d South Carolina Heavy Artillery Regiment, 3d South Carolina Heavy Artillery Regiment (1st Regulars), 15th South Carolina Heavy Artillery Battalion, 18th South Carolina Heavy Artillery Battalion (Siege Train Artillery Battalion), 1st Tennessee Heavy Artillery Regiment, 1st Texas Heavy Artillery Regiment, 3d Texas Artillery Battalion, 2d Virginia Heavy Artillery Regiment (Home Artillery), 4th Virginia Heavy Artillery Regiment, 10th Virginia Heavy Artillery Battalion, 18th Virginia Heavy Artillery Battalion, 19th Virginia Heavy Artillery Battalion, 20th Virginia Heavy Artillery Battalion, and Johnston Heavy Artillery (Virginia).

CONCLUSION

Experience in the Civil War proved that the age of the smoothbore cannon was gone. Rifled cannon could tear down the strongest forts built in the age of the smoothbore. Navies developed iron ships to replace their wooden ones, and only rifled guns were able to penetrate this new armor.

At the same time, new casting methods allowed foundries to make guns of ever-larger calibers that could fire at greater distances. This meant that the forts used to defend American ports had to be placed even further from the cities so that they could defeat enemy fleets before their ships came in range of their targets. The old brick forts placed just outside American cities were suddenly obsolete.

More durable carriages able to stand these larger guns, requiring less of the constant maintenance needed for wood carriages, were designed and made of iron. The result was that at the end of four years of war, American siege artillery and the fortifications it defended looked very different than at the beginning of the war.

SELECT BIBLIOGRAPHY

Branch, Paul, *Fort Macon, A History*, Charleston, SC, 1999

Daniel, Larry J., and Gunter, Riley W., *Confederate Cannon Foundries*, Union City, TN, 1977

Peterson, Harold L., *Round Shot and Rammers*, Harrisburg, Pennsylvania, 1969

Ripley, Warren, *Artillery and Ammunition of the Civil War*, New York, 1970

Ripley, Warren, ed, Siege Train, *The Journal of a Confederate Artilleryman in the Defense of Charleston*, Columbia, SC, 1986

Schiller, Herbert M., *Sumter is Avenged! The siege & reduction of Fort Pulaski*, Shippensburg, PA, 1995

Scott, Col. H.L., *Military Dictionary*, New York, 1864

THE PLATES

A: THE 24-POUNDER SIEGE GUN AND CARRIAGE

The M1839 24-pounder smoothbore gun was the heaviest American cannon that could be moved in the field with relative ease. A limbered piece weighed 10,155 pounds, including limber, and took 10 horses to pull. Nonetheless, the Union Army of the Potomac brought some of these guns to the front where they saw much use during the Battle of Fredericksburg. The gun was capable of firing solid shot that penetrated eight feet six inches of old earthen works at 100 yards, and almost two feet of stone and three feet of brick fortifications. The gun could also be used to fire grapeshot, canister, and spherical case shot.

According to *The Handbook of Artillery for the Service of the United States* by Joseph Roberts (New York, 1863), the 24-pounder's carriage "is similar in its construction to the field-carriage, but is joined to the limber in a different way. Projecting upwards from the limber and in rear of the axle-tree, is placed a pintle, which enters a hole made in the trail from the underside, and a lashing-chain and hook keeps the two parts together when once in position. The weight of the trail resting on the rear end of the tongue keeps this nearly horizontal, and relieves the horses of the weight of it, which, as it must be both long and heavy, is too much for the horses to carry.

"The splinter-bar is, as in field-carriages, stationary, but the traces of the next team are attached to a movable bar which is connected with the end of the tongue. The tongue is furnished with pole-chains, but no yoke, and the rest of the teams are harnessed as in field-artillery. The axle-trees are of iron, with axle-bodies of wood; which last, by its elasticity, renders the shock from the piece less direct and violent.

"On the upper surface of the cheeks, near the rear ends, are placed two projecting bolts which with the curve of the cheeks, form resting places for the trunnions, when the piece

The 150-pounder Armstrong gun at Fort Fisher, one of the best defended posts in the Confederacy, had an 8-inch bore. Note the handspikes in position to roll the gun forward to fire. (U.S. Army Military History Institute)

is in position for transportation. They are called travelling trunnion-beds. When the piece is in this position, its breech rests upon the bolster, which is a curved block of wood, bolted to the upper side of the stock. On each side of the trail, and perpendicular to it, a strong maneuvering bolt is placed to serve as places to apply the handspikes in maneuvering the carriage."

B: THE 8-INCH COLUMBIAD ON A CASEMATE CARRIAGE

The 8-inch columbiad, a standard fortification cannon, fired a 32-pound shot and required seven or eight men to fire. It was mounted on a wooden casemate carriage, resting on a roller that allowed the recoil of the gun, after it was fired, to move it back into position for reloading. Iron rails on the floor at the front and rear of the carriage allowed the gun to be moved from side to side for aiming.

According to Roberts' *The Handbook of Artillery for the Service of the United States*, the wooden casemate carriage "consists of two cheeks, joined together by as many transoms, and supported in front by an axle-tree on truck wheels, and in rear on the rear transom, which is notched to fit the tongue of the chassis. Each cheek is formed of two pieces, one on top of the other, and connected by dowels and bolts. On the underside, near the front, a notch is cut for the reception of the axle-tree, which is of oak; and nearly over the axle, on the upper side of the cheek, the trunnion bed is placed. The rear of the upper piece of the cheek is cut into steps, which give a better hold for the assembling-bolts, than a uniform slope, and give purchases for the handspikes, in elevating the piece. On the inside of each cheek, just in rear of the axle, a vertical guide is fixed to keep the carriage on the

The magazine at Battery Rodgers, in Alexandria, Virginia. Ammunition for the columbiads is stacked in the open in front of the battery. Different colors were used for different types of ammunition. (Library of Congress)

chassis. It is of wood and bolted to the front transom and axle-tree. The top of the front transom is hollowed out, to admit the depression of the piece. Behind the rear transom and at the notch cut in it, there is an eccentric roller, so arranged as to bear the weight of the rear part of the carriage, or not, according as it is thrown in or out of gear.

"Near the rear end of each cheek, and outside, a heavy trail-handle of iron is placed, and used in maneuvering the piece. On the ends of the axle truck-wheels are placed, with mortices sloping outwards in the direction of the radii, for the insertion of the handspikes in running from battery.

"The elevating apparatus consists of a cast-iron bed-plate, secured to the rear transom; an elevating-screw and brass nut; the nut being acted on by an oblique-toothed wheel, turned by a handle placed outside the right cheek."

C: A TYPICAL SEACOAST PREWAR FORTIFICATION

The American military, more concerned with a seaborne invasion of their country rather than an overland one from the west or north, built a chain of brick or stone forts around all the nation's seaports. These were usually quite similar and featured one or two levels of casemates, each pierced by guns, with a line of additional cannon on top of the fort, en barbette. A moat was generally dug around the outside of the fort, while buildings inside housed officers and men and their equipment. The open center of the fort was used as a parade ground. A shot furnace, usually placed near the casemates, was used to heat shot to fire into enemy wooden ships.

D: THE 100-POUNDER PARROTT RIFLE ON AN IRON CASEMATE CARRIAGE

Carriages made of wrought iron replaced wood carriage in U.S. Army fortifications, although the Confederates never had enough iron available to modernize their carriages in this way. Many of these carriages were still in active use in forts such as Fort McHenry, Baltimore, Maryland, as late as World War I. The Parrott on this carriage was loaded while at the end of the carriage and then it was run out to be fired over

the fortifications. Trucks with eccentric axles were used to run the gun out. The axle was turned with a wrench placed on the hexagonal end to make the trucks bear on the slide. Handspikes were then placed into holes on the truck rims to work the gun forward.

This fortification is typical of those built by both sides to defend their capital cities, Washington and Richmond, using wicker gabions and sandbags over which earth was thrown to make walls.

E: A150-POUNDER ARMSTRONG TOP, AND A 13-INCH SIEGE MORTAR AND CARRIAGE, BOTTOM

One of the most powerful weapons used by the Confederates was the British-made Armstrong cannon. They were found at Confederate forts from Vicksburg to Fort Fisher, North Carolina. These were muzzle-loaders, but rifled and highly accurate. The gun tubes had spiral coils, welded together under a steam hammer, wound around the barrel to resist the force of firing. The hoops were turned to slightly smaller diameters than the previous hoop, then expanded by heating before being dropped into place. On each side of the iron carriage was a regulating wheel that clamped the gun in place on its rails. The main problem the Confederates had with their Armstrong guns was that the ammunition they made locally didn't work well, and they had to depend on expensive imported ammunition for the best results.

The bed for the mortar was described by John Gibbon in *The Artillerist's Manual* (New York, 1860): "The bed consists of two cheeks, joined by two transoms, all cast together in the same piece. The maneuvering bolts, placed on each side, one near each end of the cheeks, are made of wrought iron, and set in the mold when the bed is cast.

"On the front transom is fastened a wooden bolster, grooved to receive the elevating quoin, which it is prescribed

Grapeshot, small cast-iron balls in a canvas bag used as anti-personal ammunition, sits in front of this 11-inch Dahlgren smoothbore gun, with a solid shot behind it. This scene was in the abandoned Confederate works at Yorktown in 1862.

should be put in position in a direction perpendicular to the axis of the piece, but is usually for convenience placed obliquely.

"Notches on the underside of the front and rear of the cheeks, give hold to the handspikes in throwing the piece to the right or left.

"Cap-squares are used with these beds, but probably only for the purpose of preventing the piece from jumping from its place when fired at very small angles of elevation, as, for instance, in ricochet firing."

In loading the 13-inch siege mortar, a cannoneer placed a powder bag in the bore. Then two men carried the round shot by means of tongs hanging on a wooden rod up the two steps to the mortar bore. A third man centered the shell in the bore, and it was then loaded into place. The men were also able to move the mortar on its wooden bed by means of handspikes that were inserted into the hole on the wheel on each side.

F: THE FORTIFICATIONS OF VICKSBURG

Control of the Mississippi River was considered vital by both sides. Vicksburg, a city halfway along it in the state of Mississippi, sitting on high bluffs overlooking the river, was a natural place for the Confederates to defend their control of the river. They spent hundreds of thousands of dollars, and used some of their best heavy ordnance, on the fortifications of Vicksburg, especially after the fall of Memphis in the north and New Orleans in the south. As designed by the chief engineer, the initial works along the river consisted of seven batteries with 18 guns placed on the 200-feet-high bluffs. According to one Confederate officer: "These batteries were located chiefly below the city; their positions were well

ABOVE **The top _en barbette_ guns at Fort Pulaski after the Union bombardment. One of the columbiads has been placed so that it might be used essentially as a mortar. (Library of Congress)**

RIGHT **The caption on this 1861 illustration from _Frank Leslie's Illustrated News_ reads: "Practicing with the celebrated Sawyer gun on the Confederate batteries at Sewall's Point, near Norfolk, Va., from Fort Calhoun, on the riprap in front of Fortress Monroe. The distance was three and one half miles, the guns were forty-two pounders (rifle), columbiads, and were the only guns then in use that could carry that distance." This essentially experimental gun, invented by Massachusetts native Sylvanus Sawyer, was a 5.862-inch rifled weapon that fired a special projectile. It was, in practice, not very successful and was phased out of service as quickly as possible.**

chosen; they had fine command of the river against a fleet coming from below." In June, 1862, another officer added that the local garrison "was engaged in strengthening the batteries already constructed, in making bomb-proof magazines, and in mounting new guns recently arrived. Several new batteries were laid out by myself on the most commanding points above the city; these were afterward known as the 'Upper Batteries.' " Despite the number and caliber of these guns, the Federal Navy sent a mockup of an ironclad, built around a barge, past the guns from the north one evening and, seeing that she took relatively little damage, was later able pass the city from either side with relative ease. The boats simply went by too fast to sustain serious damage.

G: AMMUNITION

A. An 8-inch Schenkl shell. The bottom of the cast-iron shell is covered in painted papier mâché that would safely self-destruct during firing. The shell front was hollow, and filled with gunpowder with a nose-mounted fuse that could fire on contact or at a set time. This was the same system used by all these shells. This was a U.S. design.

B. A 24-pounder Dyer shell. These shells used lead coverings, on the bottom half of the shell, that would fit into the gun's rifling when fired. This was a U.S. design.

C. A 4-inch Hotchkiss shell. Firing forced the cast-iron cup on the bottom of the Hotchkiss shell up and into the front piece, forcing the lead around the middle up and into the gun's rifling for accuracy. It was covered with a piece of greased canvas to lubricate it as it moved in the gun barrel. This was a U.S. design.

D. A 3.75-inch Sawyer shell. The Sawyer shell was entirely covered in lead which would then take the gun's rifling when it was fired. This was a U.S. design.

E. A James shell. The James shell used slanted iron ribs to spin through space for accuracy. It had lead covered with light tin plate that would expand to fit the gun's rifling when fired, and it was also wrapped in greased canvas for lubrication. On firing, gases would enter the open center of its iron ribcage, expanding and forcing the lead and tin plate into the rifling. This was a U.S. design.

F. A 4.5-inch Absterdam. This shell used a lead sabot, with a convex opening, that would be expanded by gases into the gun's rifling for accuracy. This was a U.S. design.

G. Mullane bolt. Strictly a Confederate shell, the Mullane had a convex copper sabot in its rear that was expanded by gases on firing to fit the gun's rifling. Because of the scarcity of copper in the Confederacy, the Mullane was not widely used, although examples of it have been found on battlefields of all theaters of the war.

H. Typical fuse (Hotchkiss).

Inside the defenses of Fort Pulaski, showing how Union rifled guns tore the fort's brick walls apart and made firing back impossible. (Library of Congress)

INDEX

COMPANION SERIES FROM OSPREY

ESSENTIAL HISTORIES

Concise studies of the motives, methods and repercussions of human conflict, spanning history from ancient times to the present day. Each volume studies one major war or arena of war, providing an indispensable guide to the fighting itself, the people involved, and its lasting impact on the world around it.

MEN-AT-ARMS

The uniforms, equipment, insignia, history and organization of the world's military forces from earliest times to the present day. Authoritative text and full-color artwork, photographs and diagrams bring over 5000 years of history vividly to life.

ELITE

This series focuses on uniforms, equipment, insignia and unit histories in the same way as Men-at-Arms but in more extended treatments of larger subjects, also including personalities and techniques of warfare.

NEW VANGUARD

Comprehensive histories of the design, development and operational use of the world's armored vehicles and artillery. Each 48-page book contains eight pages of full-color artwork including a detailed cutaway.

CAMPAIGN

Accounts of history's greatest conflicts, detailing the command strategies, tactics, movements and actions of the opposing forces throughout the crucial stages of each campaign. Full-color battle scenes, 3-dimensional 'bird's-eye views', photographs and battle maps guide the reader through each engagement from its origins to its conclusion.

ORDER OF BATTLE

The greatest battles in history, featuring unit-by-unit examinations of the troops and their movements as well as analysis of the commanders' original objectives and actual achievements. Color maps including a large fold-out base map, organizational diagrams and photographs help the reader to trace the course of the fighting in unprecedented detail.

WARRIOR

Insights into the daily lives of history's fighting men and women, past and present, detailing their motivation, training, tactics, weaponry and experiences. Meticulously researched narrative and full-color artwork, photographs, and scenes of battle and daily life provide detailed accounts of the experiences of combatants through the ages.

AIRCRAFT OF THE ACES

Portraits of the elite pilots of the 20th century's major air campaigns, including unique interviews with surviving aces. Unit listings, scale plans and full-color artwork combine with the best archival photography available to provide a detailed insight into the experience of war in the air.

COMBAT AIRCRAFT

The world's greatest military aircraft and combat units and their crews, examined in detail. Each exploration of the leading technology, men and machines of aviation history is supported by unit listings and other data, artwork, scale plans, and archival photography.